GW00538326

"OK! FINE!
SO MAYBE
GOD EXISTS..."

.... is a rare and original book of poetry and reflection by creative artist and poet Juliet Dawn. She writes from her own faith journey through abuse, grief, bankruptcy, loss, trauma, near death, physical debilitation and life struggles... to victory and life as an overcomer.

Through these experiences she seeks to challenge others to consider issues of life, faith , spirituality, mortality and eternity.

These are contemplations to help you find comfort in both God's love, and the divine truths that map out an eternal hope for your life. Prepare to be deeply moved as you read and experience these extraordinary pages.

It's the time for the lament
Who will write My lament?
Who will minister to My heart?
Who will share My grief?
Will you, My daughter, My precious one, dear to My heart?
As you share your pain, will you share My pain?
So few will come close to My broken heart and touch the tear that is there —- will you?
Will you dear one?
Broken hearts are not failure, they reflect My heart as much as any joy....
For My heart is wracked with the pain of a broken heart.
Tears that never end, wept for My lost ones.
My sheep ripped apart by wolves.
No shepherd to protect them.
My broken bride.
My broken church.
My broken Israel.
Will you weep with Me for My lost children?
Will you minister to My heart?
Because you have tasted of the very depths a human heart can bare,
yet remained true to me.
I can trust you dear Juliet with My pain.
Please... let Me share it with you.
You understand, I need someone who understands.
Will you?

.... I answered yes!

OK! Fine! So maybe God exists...

WELCOME, YOU THERE - BOOK BROWSER!

You may like to know, this entire book has been collated from years of steadfast writing as I have sought to navigate themes, truths and topics that God Himself has placed on my heart. After losing my own sons, God humbled me with a commission to write, and opposite you can read the very commission that God gave.

It was given to me on a white, lined piece of paper, written in biro, by a woman whom then , I did not know. She said that God had given her the exact words to write and told her to give them to me.

Considering that she didn't know my circumstances, this in itself was a miracle.

From this divinely given note, a whole prolific writing endeavour has ensued, and as you read the given words, I hope you will understand why the poetry is as it is…. emotive and deep.

Contents

OK! Fine! So maybe God exists...

Chapter 5: From the author's journey...

Chapter 6: God wants to speak....

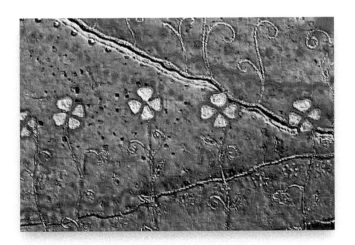

IT'S UP TO YOU...

You don't have to delve into this book if you don't want to. If you are uncomfortable with being challenged, or if you think you may be led to reconsider beliefs that you hold without really feeling prepared for that, then that's fine. Equally you may have been bought this book by someone who's looking-out for your soul, and you may not be 'ready for it' right now. Either way, it's for you to decide. I thank you for picking up this book and reading thus far.

However, such is my experience, my testimony, my journey, my understanding, my conviction, that I do believe that if you venture into the chapters within, that you may find some compelling contemplations and perhaps even some life-changing thoughts.

I myself, though born into a Christian family, have had more opportunities than most to ditch my faith and walk away from God, as well as church and faith; embittered and disillusioned. It would have been understandable and justifiable. No-one would have blamed me if I had. I have come through over 30 years (most of my adult life in fact) of trial and tribulation. So much of life's battering could have finished me off - if not 10 years of abuse, then maybe the death of my twin boys, or even the 4 miscarriages? The head on car crash and the nervous break down were pretty grim too, as were the years of night traumas and multiple near death experiences. So, believe me, I am not coming to your 'life party' with sanctimonious, 'holier than thou', ivory-tower, preachy little poems. No! I'm bringing emotive, deep experiential truths which have been born in the blackest of dark, low, raw places. Words, revelations and downloads drawn out in the depths of desperation and brokenness, and strong truths and perceptions given as hoists in my weakest, darkest times. Some, of course, have come to bear in times of joy and thankfulness, or in times of earnest seeking, but all are authentic and true: nothing contrived or artificial here. Not a speck!

> **"** I'm bringing emotive, deep experiential truths which have been born in the blackest of dark, low, raw places.

OK! Fine! So maybe God exists...

I know God has sustained me through the difficult years and that His hand has always been with me, guiding and upholding. I know He created me and placed within me a tenacious warrior spirit to keep getting up again and keep going. I know He has been my source and my Rescuer and that He loves me and tends my soul. I know so many things from my journey, but the most important is this - my earthly life may have been arduous and full of struggles, but my eternity, beyond this realm, is absolutely assured. I will reside in peace and light forever with Jesus - the One who died to save us all from the bonds of sin. Is yours assured ? Do you know?

In addition to this undeserved eternal destination, it is also with humble gratitude that I acknowledge here, that the gift of poetry that came to me in my lowest ebb, was exactly that. A gift! Divinely given and received when my own words failed to give utterance to the unfathomable tangled retchings of my soul. Only the divine and powerful anointing that was bestowed at that time could release the torrent of jumbled feelings and hence lead to what has become a prolific writing endeavour.

So, please dive in - or not!

The content and timing of this book were probably already pre-destined by the Father, and in that, you the reader, will already be known to Him and to what degree the content within will be of nurture to your soul.

I entrust your perusal of this to the Father's greater plan and to the loving hope He has for your eternal prescription; not to mention the long-planted leanings etched within, to come home to your creator! I pray you enjoy your time in these pages xx.

Chapter 1

A Little Inspiration...

 … life is full of choices; some easy, but many are difficult. Some of the most difficult life choices are often the ones that we contemplate with what seems like our whole being… heart, mind, soul and spirit. These are the places where we struggle and dialogue internally as we try and figure out how to deal with what life throws at us. We often cannot change circumstances, but we can change how we respond to them! Our decisions of purpose and attitude can determine our perspective and how life's challenges will affect us.

We do well to try and train our minds to not dwell on the negative.

OK! Fine! So maybe God exists…

WHENEVER I AM DOWN AT HEEL...

Whenever I am down at heel and lacking inner peace,
I pray for God to strengthen me with streams of joy release.
I pray for good perspectives to allow a different view,
Of life's array of challenges that have dealt a blow or two.
I look to all my blessings and I weigh their priceless worth,
And cherish all the value of the beauty here on earth,
I see the precious people that just love me beyond doubt,
And I draw from pre-lived moments when I've learnt what life's about.

I take the face of loved ones and I etch them in my gaze,
I replay special memories that no storm clouds can erase,
I find the words of wisdom oh so tenderly expressed,
By those who would support me through my journey's trials and tests.
I seize the truths I cling to and I hold them in my heart,
I reach to touch the friendships that will never drift apart,
I bring to mind the laughter and the smiles of those who care,
And I store them in some guarded thoughts, so I always know they're there.

I delve to find the riches that have made me tall and strong,
And I now see very clearly that my weakness isn't wrong,
It's just another facet of the gems that make me, me....
...... so I bravely face tomorrow, to see who I can be!!

Amen....

My Tower

I stand on trials and traumas,
I stand on conquered ground,
I stand on disappointments,
And hold to strength I've found.

I stand on smallest victories,
I stand on battles won,
I stand on jars of tears,
And problems overcome.

I stand on giant burdens
That made my shoulders strong,
I stand on words of poison;
On the ground where they belong.

I stand on rocks of malice,
Now dust beneath my feet,
I stand on cruel injustice,
That makes my tower complete!

..... From here I see the rainbow
And hear my heart beat strong,
The arm of God upholds me,
And teaches me my song...

That truth and faith and trust in Him,
Can conquer any foe!
I wonder in this life of mine,
How tall my tower will grow??

When people say ' what doesn't kill you , makes you stronger',
what they are really saying is that the process of surmounting
those life hurdles, is what builds into you the capacity to BE a
serial overcomer.

In Jesus, we have the promise of healing and restoration (Isiaiah
ch 53), and so that journey can be aided by knowledge of and faith
in these promises. What a provision this is…. freely given!

You can use each and every victory as a vantage point to see the
true person God has made you to be. It's a victor's platform onto
the next chapter of your life….

LOVE

Love that transcends all personal views,
Love that cushions the saddest of news,
Love that brings light to the blackest dark,
Love that ignites and brings hope from a spark.
Love that bears up when the spirit is down,
Love that can breach the most serious frown,
Love that turns-back a venomous hate,
It rebuffs and dilutes and can slowly negate.

Love that unites and so bridges divides,
Love that speaks value where failure resides,
Love that affirms a beleaguered soul,
Love that repairs and aspires to make whole.
Love that is patient and strives to see good,
Love that draws gold from the misunderstood,
Love that rebuilds when foundations have cracked,
It girds and supports 'til they're fully intact.

Love that subdues when a hurt turns to rage,
Love that attracts those the world won't engage,
Love that inspires; brings purpose and scope,
Love that can rescue; your friendship, its rope.
Love that is giving when someone has none,
Love that uplifts when all strength has but gone,
Love that speaks out when no voice can be heard,
It defends and protects with each well-advised word.

Love that's relentless and sees through façade,
Love that takes-in those that life would discard,
Love that unburdens by sharing a load,
Love that stands firm on the rockiest road.
Love that is medicine; it heals and it mends,
Love that brings peace when confusion descends,
Love that endorses where courage is lost,
It respects and connects and will not count the cost.

OK! Fine! So maybe God exists...

Love that embraces, when others would shun,
Love that resolves when the discord is done,
Love that just listens and gives of its time,
Love that forgives, irrespective of crime.
Love that erodes, the grey of cruel years,
Love is compassion, that wipes away tears,
Love is not touchy, it puts off dispute,
It's wise and discerning, mature and astute.

Heaven's resource – humanity's tool:
An equal share for King and fool:
An unseen force that hides its weight,
In selfless acts, both small and great,
In kindly words, both plain and grand,
In smiles that say, "I understand"….
In heartfelt hugs that show you care,
In quiet vows to lift in prayer,
In simple gifts that aim to bless,
In discipline and tenderness…
In calm response to much offence,
In hearts that seek no recompense,
In generous deeds that seek no praise,
In mild approach and thoughtful ways…
In endless faith, in boastless skill,
Enduring grace; surrendered will…

Love is what we are built for…. we are designed to love and be loved, by others and by God who created us. It is a powerful force for good, and we need to realise the potential of that positive force within us…. It can change hearts, minds and circumstances…. If not the world!!!

Love is found in many a place,
In many a hand and many a face,
It's free, and on-tap, in unmetered supply,
With limitless stocks that will not run dry…

BUT, sat in reserves it's devoid of effect,
Its God-given power is hard to detect,
It has to be channelled to be of some use,
It has to be vesseled; re-packaged; let loose.

So take all you can and then give it all out,
Use of it wisely and spread it about,
Be most aware of the power in your hand,
For this is the weapon that God himself planned.

It bears His name, it bears His might,
It comes well-versed in the "age old" fight,
So take on some battles, make LOVE the attack,
Then bless one another and see what comes back.

OK! Fine! So maybe God exists…

LOVE THAT CAN RESCUE; YOUR FRIENDSHIP, ITS ROPE

Reassuringly more tender than a mother's kiss...

OK! Fine! So maybe God exists...

What is God's Love Like?

Endlessly more vast than the sprawling skies,
Brilliantly greater than the myriads of stars,
Unendingly more infinite than the rolling galaxies,
And divinely more unfathomable than the ancient mysteries of time:
This is God's love.

Blindingly more radiant than the untethered sun,
Immeasurably higher than the eclipsing mountains,
Uncontainably deeper than the hidden oceans,
And assuredly more powerful than the fierce winds of nature:
This is God's love.

Refreshingly purer than a desert spring,
Wonderfully more beautiful than a rainbow's hue,
Comfortingly more precious than a priceless jewel,
And sacrificially more costly than all the treasures of the world:
This is God's love.

Soothingly warmer than Springtime mornings,
Reassuringly more tender than a mother's kiss,
Naturally sweeter than fragrant incense,
And earnestly more steadfast than the slow turn of the earth:
This is God's love.

Never failing,
Never ending.
Ever caring,
Ever tending.

This is God's love.

… of course, God's love for us is vast and eternal, so the limits of mere words can never convey its true essence. But if love is something that has been lacking in your own life and you find it hard to grasp…. then this poem is a good starting point …

Ok…. and breathe! Sometimes we just have to come away and come aside. Stresses of life can be overwhelming and can prevent us from seeing outside of our circumstances. Clear thinking and better perspective can often come in a moment or place of tranquillity, and that is worth remembering.

This is what I had to do. I had to carve out some quality down time in order to climb out of negativity and pressure. In that tranquil place, I found blessing, perspective, hope, faith and gratitude.

You may find God on your radar when you take time to look, review, assess… and breathe!

OK! Fine! So maybe God exists...

Tranquility

I find You in a moment; unhurried, free from time,
In beauty and in stillness; unmarred yet unrefined,
Where nature meets creation; unspoilt and untamed,
You're there in all Your glory; irreligiously en-framed.

I savour each refreshing as I catch You in the breeze,
For You've hidden heaven's echoes in the whisper of the trees.
You saturate the sky with a heavy sense of peace,
And the wispy clouds that paint it, bring soothing and release.

I try to think of nothing, but deftly, thoughts invade,
Yet here You've banned the dark ones and kindly they've obeyed.
A rest for weary minds; unladen; in respite,
Serenity brings hope and so restores your jaded sight.

Light and shade find balance, with pleasure bound in each,
And as You seek to guide me, illustrate and teach,
I look at my life differently; discernment takes a view,
For it's not just in the sunshine that You nurture and renew.

The solace of a moment in a tranquil, hidden place,
Can multiply the healing of Your balm of love and grace.
A jot in time can flourish, evolve to something more,
As You give me strength to live and give me wings to soar.

From here I see such beauty: impressive, grand design,
Invented at the makers wheel, and fused with power divine.
Each butterfly and flower, plant and tree and hill,
Narrates Your endless wonder, unmatched by human skill.

The facets of Your glory, reflect in what You've made,
There's harmony in colour, purpose in each shade.
There's wisdom in all movement; every form unique:
You're here concealed in everything, for those that choose to seek.

Where once we had an Eden; perfection, God with man,
There now exists a void; a blemish in Your plan.
So You have scattered Eden, in seeds, throughout the earth,
And here I think I'm resting.... where a seed has given birth!

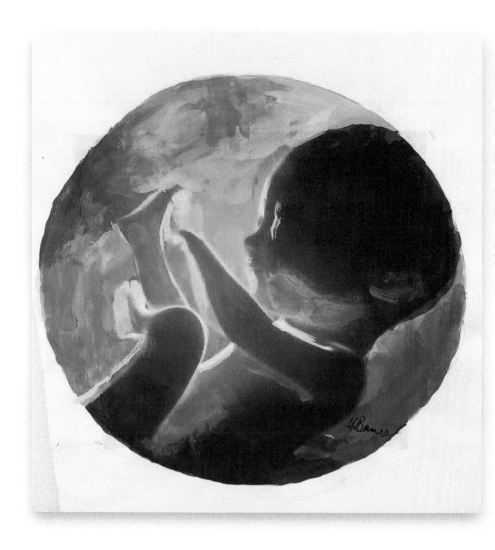

You are unique, precious, one of a kind and made by the Creator of heaven and earth! Wow.! You are not just fluke, you are a copyright of heaven. That is pretty awesome…

OK! Fine! So maybe God exists…

WHO AM I TO QUESTION?

God made me so wonderfully; I don't know how He did it?
He made just one such formula, and then He went and hid it,
Never to be copied, repeated or refined,
He loved what He had done with me, and liked what He'd designed.

He didn't mess up anything, and all was done with skill,
Made and born in God's own time, and by His perfect will,
He marked it in eternity, the day I was complete,
And ticked off all the boxes on His "Made in Heaven" sheet.

He breathed on His creation to claim it as His own,
And shared in part His Spirit, to bless the flesh and bone,
He joined this given spirit to His rich eternal stream,
So that lasting links with Father would be strong, though still unseen.

So who am I to question this creation that I am?
I am fashioned by the Father and detailed in His plan,
I am founded in the Heavens and can count this as my worth,
As I live to serve my destiny, for the time I am on earth.

Bless me today, I am wonderfully made.

Chapter 2

God cares about me..?

...God knows everything about you, and is the only one who can fix broken, emotional places that medical doctors cannot reach. That is why Jesus proclaimed that He came to mend the broken-hearted! Luke ch 4 v 18.

OK! Fine! So maybe God exists...

All He Knows…

He knows your pain, your anguish, there's nothing you can hide.
He feels your heart is breaking, the way you ache inside,
He hears your sobs of hurting, when you think no-one is there,
He's looking on and wondering… when you'll give it Him to bear.

He knows your lonely moments, when you're feeling sad and low,
He feels your sense of lostness, when the smile is just for show.
He hears each cry of sorrow, on days that never end,
He wants to fill the emptiness, He wants to be your friend.

He knows what you have suffered, He knows what you have lost,
He feels your heavy, heavy soul, as you sit and count the cost.
He hears the pangs that echo through each moment of your day,
But He waits for you to ask Him to take the grief away.

He knows how you've been treated: abuse, injustice, fear!
He's felt each frightened panic, when help was never near.
He heard your heartbeat pounding, when the fear had made you dumb..
But there's healing in His presence, and He says to you "Just come!"

He knows the things that you have done; the shame that stains your life.
He feels each twisted memory, piercing like a knife.
He hears those guilty verdicts, that haunt your tortured brain,
But He wants to wash you in His blood and take away your pain.

He knows your whirling anger that you think is justified.
He feels the weight of bitterness, that has you bound and tied.
He hears the longing of your heart, just begging to be free,
And He waits by you with open arms, saying… "give this rage to me!"

He knows of your rejection, and how you think "why me?"
He feels your sense of worthlessness and no identity.
He hears each secret wish you make, for peace and joy and love,
And it's waiting to pour down on you, in rivers, from above.

He knows the taste of pain, the crippling weight of fears.
He's felt rejection's icy grip, the smarting sting of tears.
He heard the jeers of torment as He went to pay your due,
But His arms were wide, as He hung and died, saying -
"Come, I'll make you new!"

OK! Fine! So maybe God exists...

Someone Who Cares

In times of trial and challenge
There is a friend who cares,
Who follows every detail,
Of painful life affairs.

A friend who knows of sadness,
Of hardship and of grief,
A friend who's faced the weight of loss….
And all that lies beneath.

A friend that sees your burden,
And waits close by to share
The tough and rocky passage,
Of sorrow and despair.

A friend who's tasted tears
And knows the ache of dread…
For GOD has borne what you will bear,
And trod where you will tread!

He longs to give you refuge,
Assurance, strength and peace.
He longs to lift the heaviness:
Bring healing and release.

He longs to soothe emotions,
And mix His grace with strife,
And take this journey with you,
Through this "bumpy stretch" of life.

 Jesus suffered the extremes of torture and cruelty at the hands of man and humanity. There is little of pain, grief and loss that God does not understand: God Himself in sending His Son to die, and Jesus in dying in anguish. What an amazing thing, that the divinity that saved us also endured our struggles so that we could be redeemed!!!

You Gave

What question here!
What mystery!
Was Jesus' death my sinner's fee?
What secrets lost!
What truth to tell!
Of how our souls were bought from hell!

What priceless gifts!
What sacrifice!
That took our sin and paid the price.
What humble feet
With yielded will,
That trod the path to Calvary's Hill!

What loving arms!
What servant hands!
Embraced the cross and cruel demands.
What pure intent!
What strength of heart!
Unmoved, as flesh was ripped apart!

What focused mind!
What power laid down!
To trade, for thorns, Your Royal crown!
What stricken gaze!
What desperate breath!
Led Heaven's King to certain death?

What shame You faced!
What pain You bore!
What quiet resolve, to this, endure!
What love expressed
In life You gave!
What grace poured out, the World to save!

What awesome deed!
What selfless choice!
So hell should grieve and heav'n rejoice!
What mercy flowed!
What hope to bring!
You gave, in truth, Your everything!

What peace is ours!
What freedom gained!
For Satan's power is now restrained!
What destiny!
What journey's end!
For those who would, their path, amend!

So what of this?
And what of me?
What innocence will back my plea?
What perfect claim?
What sinless thoughts?
Exclude me from God's righteous courts?

What choice remains?
What question clear?
Assess your case, then answer here...

OK! Fine! So maybe God exists...

The Road To Calvary

...truly the suffering and sacrifice of Jesus can never be overstated. What He willingly endured to pay the price for our sin and gain victory over death and evil, for the sake of our life and our eternity, is a contemplation that will last for ever….

It is Done!

Already accomplished,
Eternal, complete!
Divine Exchange,
Masterful feat!
Grace poured out,
Life giving blood,
Conquering all,
Merciful flood.

Gouging lashes,
These His stripes,
Diseases crushed,
All strains, all types.
Injurious hatred,
Unquenchable pain,
Acute, intense,
Through sinew and vein.

Limbs unhinged,
Paralysis stark,
Collapsing lungs,
Emotions, dark!
Ebbing consciousness,
Partially blind,
Spear-like thorns,
Encroach on the mind.

Violent crowd,
Contempt and shame!
Total rejection,
Lost and lame.
Naked passion,
Pure intent,
Asphixiation,
Life force spent.

Crippled limbs
Contorted bone,
Shredded flesh,
Reviled, alone.
Unjust, unfair,
Despised, accused,
Sustained assault,
Condemned, abused.

Disfigured,
Defaced,
Abandoned,
Disgraced,
Discredited,
Maimed,
Convicted…
Slain!

OK! Fine! So maybe God exists…

This was the plan, from ages conceived,
Healing released for those that believed,
Yeshua who died, complicit in scheme,
Received of your sickness, to fully redeem.

It's sealed through scripture; cannot be undone!
Victory secured, through Jesus, God's Son.
No bowing to labels, from medical notes,
Or terminal symptoms in cancerous coats.

Divine is the vaccine, for every disease,
His blood and His promise; let these be your keys!
Their power is lasting, forever and now,
Let faith be released, as your heart will allow...

Blind eyes seeing,
Deaf ears hear,
Joints repaired,
Limbs appear!
Broken, mended,
Panic calmed,
Infected, clean,
Fear disarmed!

Tumours shrivelled,
Swelling gone,
Pain abolished,
Poison, none!
Bent now straightened,
Cysts recede,
Distortion cleared,
Captives freed.

Faith ascending,
Life in flow,
Vision strong,
Dreams to sow.
Spirits stir,
Souls revive,
Mind restored,
Hope…. alive!

Defy your misgivings that scavenge for proof,
Just look to the Cross, and carry it's truth,
Deny foolish reason that seeks to crawl out,
And cry "It is done!" to each shadow of doubt.

I AM THE LORD, Your Saviour who heals,
Partake of My words as the Spirit reveals,
Draw near to My presence, prepare to receive,
Reach-out with no limit, My dear one …. believe!!

Well, if we could all pray and heal and pray and heal some more, the world would indeed be a better place. BUT the relationship between faith and healing is one that humanity is till figuring out! However, what is true and unambiguous is that Jesus died so that we could be healed and the power of His blood over sin and death, bought this victory.

The cross was a horrific, brutal, historically verified event —factual and without question. What remains uncertain is whether you accept that precious sacrifice and all the power, healing, victories and promises that come with it. It's your decision!

OK! Fine! So maybe God exists...

In the Arms of Jesus

Divinity, Purity, Truth and Love:
Stunning like crystal; serene like a dove.
What feast of treasure in beauty's disguise,
Rests still in the wonder of Jesus' eyes!

No shadow dare fall to encumber the white,
Of His royal, radiant, seamless light…
And the healing air of His holy breath,
Can purify sin and cancel death.

His shimmering aura is laden with gold:
Too fine to see, or touch or hold,
But drawing close, you are sprinkled and glazed,
As you enter His glory, transfixed and amazed!

This miracle shower of dust-like rain,
That carries His love in each delicate grain,
Beckons you forward; child-like and small,
As you yield to His reach and respond to His call.

Gentleness, Kindness, Mercy and Grace,
Flow free in the safety of Jesus embrace:
Just resting content in the nook of His chest,
Each second is savoured, each moment is blessed.

Compassion extends from each glance and each smile,
With more to its bow than to soothe you a while,
It brings security, comfort and peace,
As one brush with His gaze stirs an inner release.

Tears well up as emotions swell,
Troubles wane and fears dispel,
Yet, blinking soft, you cannot speak,
For its Jesus' tears that wet your cheek!

OK! Fine! So maybe God exists…

No sovereign act or words to charm,
Just the humbling grip of His cradling arm -
And tears that dredge and melt the pain,
With a love no heart could force or feign.

Faithfulness, Wisdom, Strength and Power:
Not subject to time nor confined by the hour,
Not polluted by pride or a selfish need,
Not tainted by sin nor diminished by greed.

This power is harnessed with patience and care,
With nurturing warmth to restore and repair;
It rests all its weight in the cup of His hands -
And each word that takes air and gently, lands.

How truly astounding! How awesomely great!
Such power and such meekness, just does not equate!
The omnipotent King with His tangible might,
Is now whisp'ring your name as He's holding you tight.

Embosomed right there with the King of Kings,
Your heart beats time and your spirit sings.
You bathe in His presence; refreshed and whole,
As deposits of joy are despatched to your soul.

> (Aside)
> Oh Jesus, my Jesus! What honour is this?
> That some never venture and others dismiss!
> What privilege lost! What favour denied!
> By those who would not come away to your side!

Compelling, Transforming, Reviving, Sublime:
Your eminent Lord waits just beyond time.
So lay down your world leaving God at the helm,
And come; be renewed in eternity's realm!

Life has taught me
that this is truly
the safest place
to be. No-one
else can offer
this compassion,
security,
protection,
promise, love,
healing, comfort,
strength and
peace. Nothing
can compare
to the comfort
of knowing and
accepting Jesus.
Period!"

Chapter 3

Life on the other side...

Heaven

Peaceful, holy, radiant, pure:
Through jewelled gates on golden floor,
Where blissful scents of angel throngs,
Attend the air with children's songs.
Each sick, miscarried, blighted soul,
Runs blemish-free, complete and whole.
And with their laughter, sunshine rays,
Ascend on high as holy praise.
Unmeasured splendour, fit for Kings,
Now opens up through angel wings,

As vibrant flowers and vivid green,
Offset this brilliant, blinding scene.
Sparkling gems adorn the street,
While mansions rise where diamonds meet,
And beauty shines from every view,
Reflecting back its light on you.
Then, as you're called before the throne,
To meet the God your spirit's known,
No words depict nor book can share,
The awesome love that meets you there...

Is this your eternal destination?

OK! Fine! So maybe God exists...

Hell

Putrid, pungent, rancid, vile:
The belly of hell presents its bile.
Tormented cries and anguished moans,
Decaying flesh and blackened bones.
Insidious worms that stake their claim,
To what was once your living frame;
Fraying joints and sinew dregs,
Were once your earthly arms and legs.
Holes for eyes and claws for fists,
Your soul a swirling, dirty mist.

Mocking laughter, piecing spears;
Demonic sport, eternal years.
Constant burning, ceaseless pain,
That sends your knowing mind insane.
A stenchful home of brimstone pits;
Consuming flames in starts and fits.
Here memories of yesterlife,
Intersperse regret and strife,
And when all fragile hope has gone,
This endless hell, just stretches on...

....OR IS THIS YOUR ETERNAL DESTINATION? (Rev 20:15)

When loved ones pass on, it is pain and sadness to the heart and soul. But when they pass on having accepted Jesus' sacrifice and recognised Him as Saviour of this sinful world…. then this is joy and comfort. I had to let my twin son Elliott go who was fighting for his life in an incubator at 4

OK! Fine! So maybe God exists…

I'll See You in Heaven...

I'll see you in heaven, my dear one,
When eternity comes to call,
Will you meet me at 'The Singing Garden',
Just beyond the shimmering wall?
Yes, I'll see you in heaven, my dear one,
When my aching soul will be free,
We can dance and embrace in the glory,
By the side of the crystal sea!

I'll see you in heaven, for certain,
When mortal flesh is released,
We will not be bound-up with sorrow,
But on joy and on laughter we'll feast.
Yes, I'll see you in heaven, for certain,
When we'll never again be apart,
And the bond that once held us in this life,
Will bring songs of deep joy to my heart.

I'll meet you in heaven .....with Jesus!!
What a glorious day will be known!!
As we share in His radiant presence,
And we praise in the light of His Throne.
Yes, I'll meet you in heaven, with Jesus!
When His love will be drying our tears,
And we'll dwell in a jubilant freedom,
And a total release from all fears.

I'll see you in heaven, no question,
When all that now hurts will have passed,
And endless days are before us,
With peace that is radiant and vast.
Yes, I'll see you in heaven , no question,
So be sure that I'll watch for that day,
When our spirits of love come together,
With no burden of grief in the way.

So, I'll see you in heaven, my dear one,
But for now you are missed here on earth,
What a beautiful legacy echoes,
Through those that were touched by your worth.
Yes, I'll see you in heaven, my dear one,
When these words will be faded and dim,
But til then we entrust you to Father,
Where together, we're united in Him.

I'll see you in heaven my dear one....
Soon it will come.

days old. I was grief stricken, but my joy was that I knew I'd see him again one day. We will dance, we will sing, we will embrace and I have this assurance! Contemplate how hollow and permanent the process of grieving is if you or the loved one have no knowledge nor acceptance of eternal life...... it is almost beyond contemplation.

OK! Fine! So maybe God exists...

Where Moth and Rust...

Light can be extinguished,
Flesh and bones decay,
A raindrop soon evaporates,
Sunsets fade to grey.
Governments will crumble,
Cities can be drowned,
Armies can be vanquished,
Kings and Queens de-crowned.
A fortune can be squandered,
Beauty only pales,

Power is often overthrown,
Strength in time just fails.
Ice-caps will diminish,
Works of art will rust,
Plants and trees will wither,
Mountains turn to dust.
Rocks can be eroded,
Landscapes re-arranged,
….But good is stored in heaven,
And there it can't be changed!

…. And so…. what we think is important of our material possessions and 'things' of the earth, will have no value or consequence in the face of eternity….. But the bible tells us that our good deeds store up treasures in heaven, and these will never be eroded (Mathew ch6 v 20). So, our choice to accept Jesus and the good we do on earth are the only things of any eternal value. Makes you think doesn't it? All the wasted effort on things that do not and will not matter in your forever after life…..

Just a Motorhome...

On earth, we are but flesh and bone, a shell in which we live,
We do not get to choose it; not ours to take or give.
A living, breathing motorhome; the vehicle we drive,
To take us on life's journey, for the time that we're alive.

The model, shape and colour scheme, we simply have no say,
We're happy if it's working as we take our chosen way.
We'd most prefer an upgrade from the heavenly parking lot,
But it's more or less a certainty; we're stuck with what we've got!

No warranty or recalls. No factory re-set switch!
No licence for a re-boot when your system shows a glitch!
No manufacturer's guarantee when faults or flaws appear!
No option for replacement when you're stuck in second gear!

There's no exchange or money back when age begins to show,
We drop our speed accordingly, so the exhaust doesn't blow!
Parts begin to wear-out and the motor starts to knock,
We start life with our foot down...... now we're barely on the clock!

Indicators drooping, paint is chipping off,
Hinges often creaking, engine starts to cough!
Radiator's leaking, plugs are getting damp,
The dashboard's looking dodgy, and so too are the lamps.

Filter needs a clear-out, the pads are wearing thin.
The tracking on the axle is the worst it's ever been!
Your bottom's thick with rusting.... and the 'big end' has now gone...
It's time to park up safely; find a verge to rest upon.

But it's our true identity that sits behind the wheel,
The spirit, soul and person, made to see and hear and feel.
We steer and we navigate with God's own Highway Code,
Yet we are all affected by what happens on the road.

The harshness of life circumstance, a rather bumpy ride,
The stress of several potholes, can affect the man inside.
A nasty brush with road rage and an accident or too,
May leave our bumper rather bent and strain our clear view.

OK! Fine! So maybe God exists...

But God has made a highway that no person can resist,
The drivers are all lovely and the cameras don't exist!
And tired, failing motors are exchanged for brand new styles,
That will never need a service: they will run eternal miles!

Good job we know our body frame is 'so not' who we are,
Whether yours is minibus or stylish sporty car,
In heaven it will be replaced, so we can live in peace,
Where all those irksome wheel clamps, will finally be released!!

So make sure you are mindful of the driver in your seat,
For he can join this holy bunch – the motoring elite!
Just see your imperfections and accept that in God's plan,
The shell is only temporary – but eternal is the man!

There really is only one life, and that's eternal; God made us that way!......
However, part of that life is lived in your mortal body on mortal earth.....
so use your time to contemplate your eternal years and how and where you'll spend them when your current motor has packed up...

If I Could come Back for a Moment

If I could come back for a moment and give out some parting advice,
I'd come with my tears of petition , and pray I'd find words to suffice.
I wouldn't need long to speak freely and give out this plea from my heart…..
To seek and to pray, don't squander each day: find Jesus before you depart.

There's always a reason to chance it, and push it away with the wind…
But bitter regret is a torment; the pain of all those that have sinned!
There's no coming back to correct it, there's no saying 'sorry' once gone,
We're given a life to find Jesus, and on last count, we only have one!

Don't leave it so long 'til the sunset, and find by the end it's too late,
Don't trust in the stars and the moonlight, and leave your forever to fate,
Don't spend your life without meaning, just living each day without aim,
Don't dwell on the raft of your failings and look to some "karma" to blame.

The end comes along all too quickly, it never is just when you think,
The day that you thought was tomorrow, has now disappeared in a blink.
The planning, the striving, the hoping, can all seem like meaningful stuff,
But dreams cannot buy you a future, no, dreams will be never enough.

Man cannot give you this wisdom, science will not portal you through,
There's never a way past the veil, well, not anything mankind can do!
Nothing will bridge to the heavens, when life in this body is spent,
Only a faith in the Father and then coming to Him to repent.

Never has anyone living, been able to see on both sides,
So my words are a desperate longing, to show you where real life resides,
It's here in the blood of Lord Jesus, it's here in the God who made you,
You'll find it in everything wholesome, in nature and love that is true.

The Bible has all of the answers, so don't put this truth on the shelf,
To read it and find your Creator, is the best you can do for yourself.
No strength that's been built in the present, can bring you back here when you've passed,
Make sure you're not wasting your efforts, for your cash and possessions won't last!!

I'd love to make clear to all people, the years that I wasted on waste,
Only my time in salvation, has brought me through death that I faced.
But…death is not more than a passing when God's loving grace has been found,
My sin wasn't on me as judgment, no longer to guilt was I bound.

OK! Fine! So maybe God exists…

It's just a thin veil to the pastures, where lightness and glory await,
There's never a sense of it fully, when we in our minds contemplate.
But I wish I could draw you a picture, to talk of it like you were here,
I'd speak of a peace and of beauty ,where all earthly ills disappear.

If I could come back for a moment , to tell of our Saviour and King,
I'd give my last breath to convince you, the biblical truth of all things,
But since its not likely to happen, that God will allow me to stray….
I'd like you to know for the record, that these are the things I would say.

It's always the truth about Jesus, about His great love and great plan,
The cross, the blood and redemption, salvation bought freely for man.
It's now about Kingdom soon coming, so my words would be urgent and short….
Don't wait for tomorrow to change things, for mine wasn't quite what I thought!!

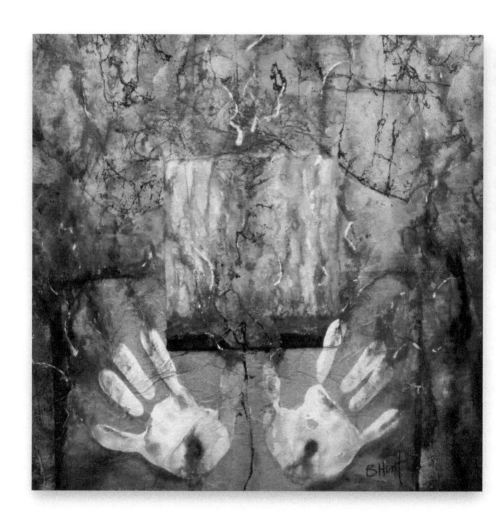

These words were
originally song lyrics;
a beautiful song with a
haunting melody, and
such a strong message.
Here, just a stand-
alone poem.

OK! Fine! So maybe God exists...

WHO'S LAUGHING NOW?

His hands were nailed, His feet impaled
A crown of thorns and a heart forlorn
A body hung and tears that stung
Yet still they mocked they laughed

Jesus, the man they crucified
Although He died
That we might live!
Your life - His loss!
Always the cross
Will hold its power
Who's laughing now?

A portrait of pain, A cry in vain
Open wounds and flesh so bruised
A darkened sky, nature wondering why
Yet, still they mocked, they laughed

Heaven or hell, who can ever tell?
Yet that's our choice, as we heed his voice
Now Lord of all, on His mercy call
To His Lordship bow... who's laughing now?

Who's laughing now?
Who's laughing now?

As the world gets darker and crazier, the time we have to choose and
consider our eternal destiny is getting shorter and shorter! This life has an
appointed end in God's map of time, and it is imperative that we make the
right decision.... To have not made a decision is to have chosen against God,
and that risk is too great when you consider what is at stake..

MILLENNIUM & ETERNITY

Christ is coming back again to re-arrange all things,
And everyone will bow the knee: all nations and all kings,
He'll bring a Kingdom reset, from which Righteousness will reign,
And this long mapped-out 'returning', will see Christ on earth again.
This prophesied redemption is the joy our future holds,
Ordained for those that know Him as eternity unfolds,
We get to rule and reign with Him and see the world restored,
And a heav'nly perfect dwelling is both promised and assured.

Eternity is endless for the saved …and for the lost,
But we were bought from hell and death, Christ paid the highest cost!
Don't risk that destination on a punt that God's not true,
But keep your faith eternal… it's the best thing you can do!

When I was younger, I talked about the biblical prophecies and accounts of Christ's return in significant future tense, but now as the world events have unfolded as per biblical foretelling, I see the times are upon us. To anyone who will take the time to read the bible account of the current days, it can leave little doubt about where we are on the world's time clock, and how close we are to Christ's return. I do not feel the need to persuade or convince, for if you read and understand…. then you will know (Matthew ch 24, Revelation ch 22). Just remains to ask yourself where you would stand in the day of reckoning that's coming? It's an important question!

OK! Fine! So maybe God exists…

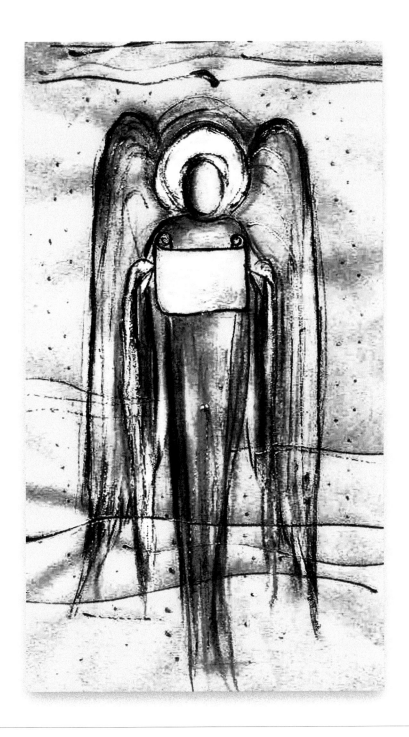

Chapter 4

Ever thought about this..?

CREATION

Creation begs the question,
How came I so refined?
Did such sophistication,
Just happen undesigned?
Did space and time self manage,
So perfectly aligned?
Did light and dark appear,
By luck and chance combined?

Did every tiny atom,
Create itself a glue,
To stick to other particles,
That also made some too,
And by some secret language,
Make sure all cell-life knew,
That they would make the universe,
By forming, bang on cue!

By all their thinking efforts,
Did atoms form a plan,
And brainstorm evolution,
To one day make a man?
But first they found a conscience,
And development began;
A complicated set-up,
To resist, respond and scan!

Did cell life form in structures,
With features quite unique;
And prototypes emerging,
As something rather sleek!?
With super-charged receptors,
(Like ears, so to speak),
And flexible and thinnish skin,
... So contents wouldn't leak?

The mission thus successful,
Did atoms then contrive,
To set about inventing,
And bringing stuff alive?
A billion different species,
NOT all that would survive,
And climates, skies and weather...
Ensuring life would thrive?

Some types were just made static,
And some would move around.
Some things would fly above them,
And some go underground!
Some life would walk the planets,
To earth and sea be bound,
But later they were modified........
For several species drowned!!

Did then these new formations,
Imagine greater scale?
Things had to work in cycles,
If life was not to fail.
So, did they summon systems,
And all that would entail...?
Boy! Things were getting tricky
On this reproductive trail!

Did clever little atoms,
Become a world of stuff,
Hot and cold and tepid,
Prickly, smooth and rough?
Vast and microscopic,
Fragile, porous, tough:
From huge galactic stratospheres,
To belly button fluff??

OK! Fine! So maybe God exists...

Creation had a crisis:
Her thinking cells were beat!
If she hadn't self-invented,
Then, she'd have to see defeat!
She looked at all her beauty,
This amazing complex feat,
And saw in just one moment
That her thoughts were incomplete.

She'd thought that it was foolish,
To believe that she'd been made.
But this was far more senseless,
... This "self-evolve" charade!
She mused and looked to heaven,
And there she saw God's hand,
With soil beneath His fingernails,
Stretched-out to tend the land.

Right there she heard God's heartbeat;
She recognized the thud –
The rhythm of her seasons,
The sense of all her good.
She wanted then to shout it,
And only wished she could,
That she'd recognized her maker
..... and she finally understood!

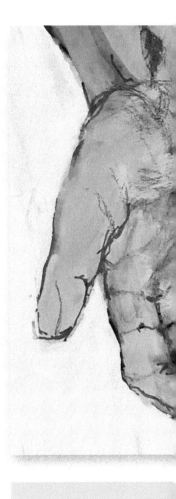

Seriously right….. self-creation or evolution doesn't even make sense in the context of the laws of the world around us that we have spent years learning…… it just isn't feasible that things make themselves out of nothing! Really????? Seems to me like even the man (Darwin) who first created the idea and notion (no more that that) also thought it was crazy and refuted the idea before he died. Humanity has a long history of using science to try and disprove God and creation. Latest scientific reports are now seeing that creation is so complex, so intricate, so intelligent, that it could not have happened without design or by coincidence.

Do you believe everything that you have been told in your life, right or wrong, or have you used you own critical insight and research to fully investigate the truth…?

OK! Fine! So maybe God exists...

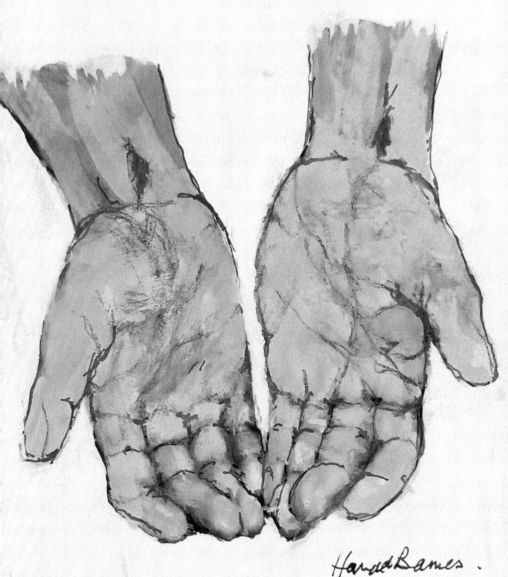

Harold Barnes.

OK! Fine! So maybe God exists...

The Wonderment of Birth

Through life we love occasion; we define our years this way,
We laugh and cry and dance and sing through every milestone day!
But what more cause to celebrate, than a brand new child on earth?
The preciousness of new-born life, and the wonderment of birth!

What happiness, what blessing, what gratitude and hope!
What purest, truest sentiment! What dreams with endless scope!
What tender rich emotion which abounds for all to see…..
That you, through God's unique design, have made a "mini me".

What privilege and honour, for this child that you have grown,
Was knitted by the Father and from eternity was known,
So we can't help but share your joy by thanking God above,
That He arranged this miracle and sealed it with His love.

We join with you to seal that love and gird this life in prayer,
We bless this soul with truth and light to shine out everywhere,
We ask protection always and we raise a toast to say,
May God show favour year on year and forever guide your way.

I think that birth, existence and life-force have been taken for granted over
the years, and that indoctrinations about life, family, community, national
identity etc. have taken the emphasis and wonder from this miraculous
concept. Let's recap; this is an unseen life-force giving life energy and breath
into flesh and bone that is grown inside a woman's body! Its amazing! It's a
miracle! It's not science….. It's a complete divine wonderment! Don't let the
world's tendency to underplay creation and steal the joy of the incredibly
amazing gift of life, blind us to the miracle that is in front of our eyes.

You can use this at a dedication or Christening ; feel free to share.

When Babies Fly to Jesus...

When babies fly to Jesus and leave this sullied earth,
In sleep, in wombs, in sickness or seconds after birth,
There are no words to speak the pain, there are no ways to say,
The vast and total brokenness left gaping on display.

The innocence of fragile life, blown out and beyond reach,
The hopes and dreams of future things left flailing in the breach.
No hand can touch, nor grasp return… the breath, the life, the source….
No tears can melt the veil, as the soul now flies its course.

What all-consuming sorrow is left to those who mourn,
What limitless affliction when hope and joy lay torn,
What searing, aching, longing, infects the startled heart!
What bitter, tameless sadness will tear your peace apart!

BUT stay a moment longer to see what I have learned,
It's a knowledge found through anguish, and not easily discerned!
No deepest grief can buy it, no darkest depth can show,
The wonder of eternal truth that I have come to know.

Born-out in aching chasms, in pools of loaded tears,
Cemented through the trauma and so many desperate years,
Established in the hurting of the very black abyss ……
Is a truth adorned in comfort and assurance clothed in bliss.

As souls fly on to Jesus, their suffering falls away,
Their little lives are weightless… in shimmering light they play.
Bereft of any earthly plight and void of any strife,
A spotless perfect body, and a pure unspoilt life.

Light and love and goodness, reflect off angel wings,
And eyes and voices lift in praise as all of Heaven sings.
Laughter meets with music and ascends with heavenly sounds,
Where liberty brings freedom's dance as innocence abounds.

OK! Fine! So maybe God exists...

At the funeral of our twin boys, Louis and Elliott, we played "Fly" by Celine Dion: it was incredibly moving and poignant. But the echoes and sentiments of that song have become more animated and detailed in my core as the years have passed. Now I have a full pictorial video of this event in my heart and in my head. This glorious perception is what I share with you here......

There Jesus calls the children and brings them to His side,
To love them all eternally, and forever they'll reside….
In glorious perfection, away from hurt or stain,
Now safe from earthly trappings and escaping mortal pain.

This life is bent on sorrow, this world is growing dim,
God's purposes are hastening, and there's nothing without Him….
The One who sent His Son to die to deal with all of sin…
And through His blood and sacrifice we all can enter in.

The day is soon approaching when the Lord will show His hand,
And my spirit leaps and leaps again to see what He has planned,
When an all-out celebration, just beyond the skies and moon,
Will mark a D-day party with our children lost too soon.

Too good they were for this life: to Jesus they have flown,
Carefree from darts and arrows, and the bumpy life we've known,
But banish not the knowledge of this One who bore the cost......
As they dance with Him 'til D day...... our babies who were lost.

There Came a Day in Heaven...

There Came a Day in Heaven…
…When grief consumed the air,
When heavy lay the sorrow,
And thick, was spread despair.

God's heart was sorely troubled,
His body ached with strain,
He wiped His cheek in secret,
And sat, to nurse the pain.

He slumped His face down slowly,
And caught it in His arm,
Then swept His brow most gently,
And breathed a silent calm.

"My Father", Jesus ventured,
As close He drew beside,
For no more could His silence,
Conceal what was inside.

"My Father", He repeated,
"Please tell what burden grows.
I know the world is wicked.
I know what evil flows."

"I know that this has grieved You,
That much You can't disguise,
I share this pain My Father…
… Once more it's man's demise!"

"But Father, there is something,
Which You have dared not say.
It far exceeds man's wickedness,
And ails You night and day."

"Father, hear Me tender,
We need to talk, we must!
Please spill Your heart with knowledge,
You have My ear, My trust."

Well God just eyed Him briefly,
And softly took His hand,
Whilst in His heart He cried out,
And hoped He'd understand.

"My son" He said "My precious,
You're loved beyond all doubt!
And that great depth of feeling,
Is what My pain's about."

Jesus searched His countenance,
For meaning He'd not heard,
And though His lips were waiting,
He could not say a word!

He summoned all His trusting,
And brought it to His eyes,
To nod a gentle prompting,
With strength both warm and wise.

"My Jesus" God continued,
"I will try to explain.
Just cast a glance down earthwards,
And see man's sin again!"

"The world is worse than ever.
Few men will stand for good,
And though My laws are flouted,
This time – there'll be no flood."

"Of course", responded Jesus,
"This promise You have made.
Your Word endures forever,
Though time and space will fade!"

OK! Fine! So maybe God exists…

Again there came a moment,
When something passed between…
…The love of Son and Father,
Was felt, but went unseen!

"You cannot know My grieving,
To speak to You of this."
Were next the words God uttered,
Then held His gaze in His.

His voice was thin with trembling,
His look was showing pale,
But God was drawing purpose,
His plan to now unveil.

"I see no other option,
But someone else take blame,
For all that man be judged for,
For every sin and shame!"

"For every act of murder,
For every heinous deed,
For all the future Kingdoms,
Of power and lust and greed."

"For every lie and slander,
For malice and deceit,
For every man that's blasphemed,
Or bowed at idol's feet."

"For every moral downturn,
For every nation's guilt,
For every cruel injustice,
There's blood that must be spilt!"

God looked through blinks and tears,
To answer now His son,
But Jesus, also crying,
Now knew what must be done!

God took a seconds respite,
To map His words with care,
For now, He'd send for slaughter,
The son He longed to spare.

"The punishment is vile,
For justice claims its due.
The sin of all the ages,
I fear, must fall on You!"

God expected horror,
To fall from Jesus' face:
A deluge of emotion,
And fumbled words of grace.

But Jesus touched so deeply,
By all His Father's woe,
Just smiled at Him and whispered,
"My Father, I will go!"

With glassy eyes now weeping,
And love and grief entwined,
He spoke out one more promise,
With what courage He could find.

"I'll give each soul a future:
To reign with You on High,
But they must choose to love You…
For them… I'll choose to die!"

Yes…. there came a day in Heaven,
When Jesus changed the Script,
His heart of pure compassion,
Left Satan's mandate…… stripped!

WHEN GRIEF CONSUMED THE AIR...

OK! Fine! So maybe God exists...

There certainly must have been a day in heaven...... but who really knows if it went like this or not. One thing is for sure..... it was a huge sacrifice for God to send His Son, but He loved the world so much, that He made a way!..... John ch3 v 16

The True Cross

A day given over and set aside,
For the worlds of evil and good to collide.
A day whose purpose could not be restrained,
It was destiny bound, as God had ordained.

A time that was poised to change history's course:
A breath drawn 'cross nature, as dread sapped its force.
A time that was marked from eternity's birth,
When heaven's victory would pierce the earth.

A moment engraved in the planning of time:
The payment for ev'ry sickness and crime.
A moment when freedom, in anguish, was bought,
Creation trembled and wretched at the thought.

A scene now distorted and misunderstood,
For we soften the faces and mop up the blood,
A scene of unwatchable cruelty and pain,
As it fell to One Man, our hope to regain.

A man in innocence bearing our guilt,
Yet choosing His heavenly blood to be spilt.
A Man whose purity thwarted sin,
Untainted through life, 'til His body gave in.

A body of flesh, so ripped and torn,
Defaced by men, with Satan's scorn.
A body maimed then nailed on display,
So the World could witness what happened that day.

A way now made by this awesome plan,
When cringing injustice brought grace to man.
A way forged to Heaven – as Hell was rocked,
For its hold was broken; its shackles unlocked.

No half-hearted gesture, no easy ride,
It was brutal and grim as our Saviour died,
No silhouette cross; elegant and neat;
It was stained with blood from His hands and His feet.

Ok, so let's talk plainly. Easter was originally a pagan festival that was about worship of the fertility goddess (Ishtar) and child sacrifice. Sorry, but this is true. Not talked about, but true. The Church/State a long time ago highjacked this festival as an alternative to Passover, and sought to impose some religious symbolism and sentiment on the feast day. Hence now things have got watered down, with barely a nod to anything that looks like an authentic remembrance of the cross; Easter is slowly resorting back to its pagan origins. Here, I invite you to take a moment to see and understand the true cross of Jesus that actually happened at Passover ....

OK! Fine! So maybe God exists...

For God so loved the world that He gave His only Son.

And on the third day, nature let out its breath,
For Jesus, in glory, defeated death.
He rose from the tomb, a captive no more,
And heaven shone-down every smile from its store.

So this was Easter, how far have we come?
From history's truth to the hot cross bun!
From Jesus' death and all its ills,
To eggs and lambs and daffodils.

We've airbrushed our Saviour, we've airbrushed the cross,
We've airbrushed the day from all its dross,
So let's, just this once, remember the price,
That was paid for us by God's sacrifice.

But What About..?

What about my Grandma, who sadly died of cancer...
..and my work mate whose son passed on...still waiting for an answer.
And my friend Jane whose husband left, now can't afford her flat.
She's the kindest person I ever met; she didn't deserve all that!

What, pray tell, of Africa, I just don't understand,
Why God doesn't send a miracle and irrigate the land?
You see the stricken faces – hunger, famine, disease.
Why doesn't God save children at least, can someone tell me please?

What about Northern Ireland, where so many souls were killed,
..and nature's earth disasters where blameless blood is spilled?
There's story after story of people's lives - just wrecked!
Why doesn't God just warn us, then we'd know what to expect?!

What about the Middle East - Palestinians and Jews?
Brutal, bloody killings are always in the news.
Suicidal bombers… then revenge to fix the score.
It's murder in religion's name – is this a 'holy war'?

What about 9/ 11, surely God could have intervened,
Was He simply just not listening as the victims burned and screamed?
The evil of that fateful day just all seems so unfair,
I wonder – would God have stopped it, if I too had been there?

OK! Fine! So maybe God exists…

And what about my own life, it's a non-stop woe propeller....
I could write a book on problems – it'd be a sure best-seller!!
Bankruptcy, hurt and rejection; disappointment, illness and shame.
So why do I need Jesus, when He's the one I blame?!

How can I be a Christian with so much unexplained?
My head's so full of questions; life's mysteries engrained!
Why should I follow Jesus, with so much I don't understand,
So I prefer to live in guiltless sin and stick my head in the sand!

BUT WAIT..

Do you understand relativity, Einstein and his theory?
And do the laws of genetics not leave you with a query?
Do you understand micro- physics and how the oceans flow?
... just because you can't explain it, doesn't mean that it's not so!

So what about this Jesus whom history confirms?
He lived and died and rose again, to give you better terms:
Instead of dying in your sin, He paid the price for you,
Love drove Him to this master-plan... so now what do you do?

What about eternal life, a question we all must face?
Satan claims your weary soul; unless you accept God's grace.
Don't waste your life on questions, when your destiny's at stake.
Hear God's voice – and make your choice – but choose well for goodness sake!!

Excuses! We all have lots of excuses! Tons of them! Excuses will not mean didly squat to
your Creator if you don't accept the sacrifice of His Son that He provided. Our sin would
have meant punishment for us and judgement, but Jesus took the sin, shame and
judgement so that we could avoid inevitable consequences. Ultimately excuses will take
people to Hell, with lots of other folk who also lived in their excuses. It isn't 'being bad'
that lands you in Hell, its not accepting the truth of Jesus as advocate, Saviour, sin-taker,
Redeemer and Risen King. Its not controversial, its just that the world has sold people a
lie of heaven after death. The truth is, this is only for those that accept Jesus....

AT ANY ONE TIME...

At any one time someone dies of aids,
And another self-harms with razor blades.
At any one time someone cries to sleep,
As they're put in to care – too hard to keep!
At any one time a heart is broken,
And words of despicable cruelty are spoken.
At any one time a schoolboy is bullied,
And a view of the world is besmirched and sullied.

At any one time someone takes their last dose,
Of crack cocaine or something gross.
At any one time someone's vein is injected,
And a needle passed on, exposed and infected.
At any one time a life is trapped,
And a suicide victim's neck is snapped.
At any one time a freedom is sold,
And another, neglected; too frail and old.

At any one time someone good, goes bad,
'Cos they've witnessed their Mum beat-up by Dad.
At any one time someone falls to their knees,
And begs for their life with desperate pleas.
At any one time a body is battered,
And the bones of a blameless victim are shattered.
At any one time a murder's committed;
A family bereft and fleetingly pitied.

At any one time someone's labelled a freak,
And a greedy soul exploits the weak.
At any one time someone's left for dead,
Judged for their skin or something they said.
At any one time a tribe is erased,
A township torched and a village blazed.
At any one time there is genocide,
And the homeless flee with nowhere to hide

OK! Fine! So maybe God exists...

At any one time someone's turfed on the street,
A beggar dies hungry; no food to eat.
At any one time someone beds in the dust,
And an orphan runs aimless with no-one to trust.
At any one time a feud kills a child,
And terrified kids are abused and defiled.
At any one time a baby is taken,
And somewhere a frightened infant is shaken.

At any one time a trust is betrayed,
An innocent maimed by gun or grenade.
At any one time a bomb is fused,
And a chemical poison, prepared, to be used.
At any one time someone sites their aim,
On innocent blood and corporate blame.
At any one time someone grieves for the dead,
And revenge sits proud on many a head.

At any one time man's hate will flare,
And a tortured soul befriends despair.
At any one time, young hopes are snatched,
As plots of "hell on earth" are hatched.
……….. Yet, on we go, our peace infringed,
Our freedom speak, yet more impinged,
And God bends down to hear our cry,
But we battle with dark and dodge His eye!

So, please don't think that this world is OK,
For around us is tragedy, crime and decay;
We need God's hand and we need it fast,
Less the chance for redemption, be long since past!...

And as we reflect on our own share of woe,
Consider the other ten thousand or so,
Who live in ruin, aware of the fact,
That only their thoughts and prayers are intact.

It's time for action! It's time for change!
The days are short and dark and strange.
So, pray for lost souls and Godless lands,
When we next book time for our list of demands.

And let's think of the starving and those without hope,
When we next rail at God, saying, "Lord, I can't cope!"

This world is run by the filthy minds and intentions of the evil elite, and they do not care a jot about you, your life or your soul. Its time now to wake up and see the story and

OK! Fine! So maybe God exists…

see their plot. It doesn't end well for "us" in the writings of their plans. God is the only answer for humanity and for the world........ everything else is fake. All is not and will NOT be ok without God's intervention and masterplan!"

CHRISTMAS ALL WRAPPED UP!

There is an ancient story, unboxed this time of year,
We wheel it out each Christmas, with the tinsel and the beer:
A man, a girl, a baby, a barn, some sheep and beast,
An evil King, some shepherds and three wise men from the east.

Year on year we're fed it; drearily it's told,
There is no special magic as we hear the plot unfold.
From childhood's early memories, to… just a year ago,
It's word for word repeated; solemn and rather slow!

Indifference and tradition have worked in hand with time,
To undertake the dealing of a subtle kind of crime;
They've stolen all the meaning from the tale of Jesus' birth,
They've drained it of its wonder and they've stripped it of its worth!

And yes, familiarity, has played its part as well,
In sifting out the power from the story that we tell.
We've heard each verse so many times, we've ceased to be impressed,
By how God sent His Son to earth and how the World was blessed.

Not only are we immunised to each amazing fact,
And really seldom awestruck by God's mighty, selfless act,
We've also buried Christmas – in its truest Birthday sense-
Beneath the decorations and a month of great expense!

There's baubles, trees and candles and lights of every sort,
There's pudding, cake and chocolates all begging to be bought,
There's penguins, snow and glitter, Santa and his elves,
There's Christmas gifts for everyone, just spilling off the shelves!

There's packaging and paper; expensive, fancy tags,
There's gold and silver wrapping; a vast array of bags,
There's bows and bells and ribbon; there's every size of box,
There's a way to gift wrap everything from champagne flutes to socks!

But we have gift wrapped Christmas, like parcels round the tree,
In dazzling, shiny paper, so people cannot see,
…what's hidden on the inside of that present lying there,
And really it's a precious, timeless gift for all to share!

OK! Fine! So maybe God exists…

Yes, Christmas is another one…..
a celebration, a feast, that God did
not instruct or instate. No wonder it
has got confused, infected, diluted
and estranged…. Yes, its sliding
back to its pagan roots! Jesus was
likely born in Spring, and so this is
yet another false feast sold to us by
the ruling powers. 25th Dec was a
birthday, feast day for a pagan god
(Mithra), and so now it is indeed a
festival and time of merriment, but
one that has little to do with the
true celebration of Christ's birth.

So, let's unpackage Christmas… let's peel those layers back.
Let's ditch the pagan trimmings and dispense with Santa's sack.
Let's lay aside the crackers and shovel through the snow,
'Cos at the heart of Christmas, there's a truth the World should know.

The Jesus that was born that night, grew way beyond the story.
A child, a man, a sacrifice, who now resides in glory!
He did this to redeem us, by paying sin's high price.
Yes, awe inspiring love has paved our way to Parardise.

But there is something in return that God wants us to give.
It won't cost you a penny…. but it will change how you live.
He doesn't just want "thank you" and a nod when we remember.
He wants your love, your heart, your life, from now….. 'til next December!

So, how would we "do" Christmas, if God himself came down?
Do you think he'd dress as Santa; switch the lights on in your town?
This year let's go much deeper; let's exercise our choice.
Let's re-instate the Christmas in which God has got a voice!!

Every Second Matters...

Every second matters,
Every minute counts,
Life is slowly ticking by in God's pre-planned amounts.

The days are breathing heavy,
They splutter and they lurch,
The end of time is clear in sight, and we're asleep, Oh church!

The hours now are numbered,
The years remain but few,
Has yet the sense of urgency, to full descend on you?

God's given out His warnings,
By prophet, hand and pen,
He long foretold the crucial signs of how and what and when.

Beware the age is waning,
It's later than you think,
The anti-Christ will claim his throne before the World can blink!

Players are positioned,
Prophecies are lined,
We're living end-time scripture, yet we act as though we're blind!

Bible views we elbow,
And Godly ways we mock,
It's edging close to midnight now on God's prophetic clock!

Yes, every word now matters,
Each decision counts,
Life is slowly ticking by, as fast the darkness mounts......

OK! Fine! So maybe God exists...

The world is in crisis! Humanity and society are not just poorly, but desperately sick! In a desperate bid to brush off a terminal diagnosis, the global elite have turned up the wick on tyranny and control; but God's plans are immovable. The diagnosis cannot be reversed and God's Kingdom reset is closer than close to midnight. Time is almost up, and if you have eyes to see 'the times', you probably already sense this. Keep your eyes open and your heart searching for both truth and the 'decision crossroads' ahead…

Chapter 5

From the
Author's Journey...

LIFE

Life with its torrid leanings,
Has come nipping at my senses,
Wrapped up with mis-shaped meanings,
And stripping my defences.

I search for sound instruction,
To deal with what is thrown,
But these bullets of destruction,
Confound all I have known.

Thoughts jostling for position,
Which one will take the lead?
I'm bound by indecision,
Though I pray and beg and plead.

No answers staring wisely back,
No certainty in view.
Where is the cure for what I lack?
Or advice for what to do?

A jumbled mess of feelings,
An array of splintered goals.
A mix of different dealings,
Each vying for my soul.

Wisdom waits, obscured,
Hiding without a trace.
There waiting 'til my fate's assured,
Before he shows his face.

Frailty fights confusion,
In the pain of standing still.
Definites are an illusion.
And the truth's a bitter pill.

I'm stood on the brink of tomorrow,
With a pocket full of choices,
Swaying in storms of sorrow,
On a raft of inner voices.

"Where's my strength and resolution?
Where's my surety of mind?"
Seems the force of life's pollution,
Unhinged them far behind.

"Where's my clarity and boldness?
Where's my confidence and grit?"
Seems the years have brought on oldness,
And they've tried to stifle it.

OK! Fine! So maybe God exists...

..... THERE'S MORE

"Where's my easy, strident manner?
Where's my positivity?"
Seems that trouble broke my banner,
And took the best of me.

"Where's my optimistic sayings?
Where's my all–defiant stand?"
Seems my black and white is greying,
And so's my hope for all I planned.

BUT, there's destiny yet veiled,
For this life that's taken hold,
And as I crumble, limp, de-railed,
God's master plan unfolds….

He's seen my worthy assets,
That I feel have all but gone,
And He's weighing up the facets,
On every precious one.

He's mending chinks and scratches,
Polishing every scuff.
He's tending weakened patches,
Where life has been too rough.

Improving and rebuilding,
Every kink that makes me, me,
And sourcing special gilding,
Of the rarest quality.

See, God's got more in waiting,
Than to fix my wounded zeal.
He's ditched my flimsy plating,
And He's girding me with steel!

Mended, strengthened, repaired,
And set back on my track.
Restored, enhanced, prepared,
To face the next attack.

No, God's not left me flailing,
Sea-logged and barely afloat.
He's just teaching me more about sailing,
And upgrading my war-torn boat.

So I choose to trust in the Father's hand,
While life itself is my foe,
For with ev'ry trial , I don't understand….
I live, I learn, I grow.

The journey of life has not been easy or kind, but with God's help, I have persevered and endured. Faith has been my constant, family have been my blessing and support. and my tenacious character has made me just too stubborn to give up. God has fashioned the very best of me though life's trials and traumas and His promises and purposes have upheld me through the darkest times….. I am a better repurposed model for having allowed God to use life's journey to shape me to be more like Him.

OK! Fine! So maybe God exists…

Blackness Surrounding

Blackness surrounding,
Darkness pervades,
Numbness that hurts,
Grief in swathes.
Lost in the aching,
Pulled down by the pain,
Drowning in tears,
Again and again.

Deafening thoughts;
They sting and they smart.
Breathtaking sadness,
Infecting your heart.
Shock brings in choking,
In vice-like grip.
Loss brings in poison,
Drip by drip.

Fear in waves,
With torrent-like force.
Death with its sting,
Intent on its course.
The lash of torment,
Bruising your mind.
Haunting delusions,
Cruel and unkind.

Crushing shadows,
Bear down on your soul.
Fluttering images,
Come not to console.
Visions of evil,
Parading its glee.
Flashes of nightmares,
Now reality.

Surviving each minute,
Grasping at dreams.
Your life in shreds,
Spilling out at the seams.
Self-pity beckons,
Desperation looks on.
Hopelessness loiters…
Hoping faith is now gone!

BUT, faith long implanted
Has roots that go deep,
It nurtures your strength
In your rest and your sleep.
Puts belief in your heart,
Truth on your tongue,
Reminding your spirit,
To whom you belong.

It quells the anger
That rages inside.
It repairs those seams
That have opened so wide.
Tames the lies
That ring in your ears,
And absorbs the hurt
Of a million tears.

It re-focuses eyes
To eternity's plan.
Where you say "I can't",
A voice says "You can",
And through the debris
Of brokenness,
A light will emerge,
To heal and to bless.

OK! Fine! So maybe God exists…

A light strong and steady,
Enduring and warm.
It can't be extinguished,
It weathers the storm.
Always shining,
Through chasms of doubt,
Till the darkness subsides
And the blackness, goes out!

Please don't think that I don't know lostness, despair and blackness… because I do! Utter bereft, aching, jumbled blackness! This does not afford me greater status or a badge of honour, but it does mean that you can't say to me:
" You don't know what its like, it's alright for you."
I am living proof that God can uphold you, repair you, love you, guide you in the darkest times, even when you cannot see the way out or the way forward. Here's my absolute game-changing truth—God always uses the blackest tunnels to bring forth the brightest diamonds... if you let Him. No trauma is wasted if you entrust your journey to Him !

After four miscarriages and two lost boys (one dying in my arms, the other dead in my arms), my heart overflowed with gladness when Max (who always lives up to his name) came along. He was a 'God-orchestrated miracle', as the conception and gestation mirrored EXACTLY to the day, the twins' pregnancy. I saw and knew God's handprint all over every aspect of this pregnancy and this gave me peace, hope and gratitude. This was a moment of restoration in life's balancing scales, AND of course, another miracle!

NOW I KNOW...

How truly grateful can one heart be,
That you reserved this child for me?
How long in the planning? How long in design,
So this true gift could be packaged as mine?
How long did this secret sit close to Your chest,
So You could bless me with Your heavenly best?
And how could You not, share hints of Your plan,
When You knew all along about this little man?
So playful, so happy; so full of delight!
Smiling, contented, tactile and bright!
Laughing and looking with love-filled eyes.
A spirit born gentle, mature and wise.
Have angels protected some special mould,
Reserved for the Great, since the Saints of olde?
And have unique parts of this precious stock,
Been guarded through years under key and lock?
The spirit, the soul, the flesh, the bone,
Were assembled in thought, before they were grown.
It defies all belief; it blows my mind,
That this perfect form, to me, was assigned.
BUT NOW I KNOW LORD...
You wrote this whole chapter before my first breath,
For You knew this blessing would balance out death.
So, forever I'm humbled, that my little boy,
Was born of Your schemes Lord, to bring me such joy!!

He gives beauty
for ashes,
the oil of joy
for mourning,
the garment of praise
for the spirit
of heaviness···
Isaiah 61·3

OK! Fine! So maybe God exists...

Beauty for Ashes

Many times, many ways,
As the path through life we trace,
We can find the ashes life has left behind.
Traumas, trials, failure, loss,
Each has left their mark,
But seeds of love God planted,
Then, keep pushing through the dark.

So come the spring,
Through everything,
God's purposes will bring...

Beauty for Ashes,
Joy instead of tears,
Strength exchanged for weakness,
Faith replacing fear.
Where we were shallow,
Maturity appears,
Even threatening storm clouds,
Slowly start to clear.

Then trembling, trusting, even though its hard,
I must learn to give the ashes and the places life has scarred,
Into the hands of the God of miracles,
So I can learn to live again.

"

This was the promise of God. Beauty for Ashes. No wait.... this IS the promise of God (Isaiah 61 v 3). If you can find the courage and faith to give Him the ashes of your life, He will bring beauty from them. This book is part of the beauty that my life has now found.... because I gave over my ashes. Please examine these words and let them touch you—these were words forged together by my Mum and I—after hearing God's promise. And if you can't read them with a free heart, then perhaps go to YouTube and find the song that this became.... I hope and pray the words will give you deep hope.

DESTINATION TROUBLE

Destination trouble, there's a storm on the way.
Will you stand or will you fall
When the sky turns blackish grey?

Destination trouble, there's a spearhead poised and raised.
Will you lift up high your shield of faith
Or stand confused and dazed?

Destination trouble, there's a raging bull around.
Will you engage your enemy
Or be trampled to the ground?

Destination trouble, there's a hunter on the loose.
Will you fight and win against all odds
Or be captured in his noose?

Destination trouble, there's a tempest gaining pace.
Will you anchor to the word of God
Or be blown from place to place?

Destination trouble, there's a lion seeking prey.
Will fear unhinge your gallant stride
When his footsteps come your way?

Destination trouble, but no matter what I face,
I'll put my hand in Jesus' hand
And use His strength and grace!

OK! Fine! So maybe God exists...

If you believe God doesn't exist, then why do we curse Him, saying "Oh God!"? Instead of cursing Him and at the same time dealing with the tribulations of life alone, let God be your strength and anchor.

If you're going to, on one hand acknowledge Him by cursing Him for life's adversity with verbal throw-away blame, you may as well turn that around for your own good. Talk to Him directly and ask Him to show you Jesus, His Son, and then ask Him to be your strength and shield. This has been my security and confidence through all of life's troubles!

MIRACLE

Funny how life turns out sometimes when you're steadily pressing on,
One minute you have joy and peace,
>The next…. it's all but gone!
>Your peace has turned to fear,
>And your joy has turned to pain….
>It's like when clear and sunny days are ambushed by the rain.

Funny how life turns out sometimes, when you're cruising unawares,
We forget the road, though often smooth,
Is also laid with snares.
What first we see as golden…
Can quickly turn to grey….
And a treasure that you're holding,
Can soon be snatched away.

Funny how life turns out sometimes, when your plans are laid ahead,
Then circumstances all conspire,
To bring on only dread!
Your way, that once was certain,
Is suddenly obscured,
And any precious blueprint,
Is now well and truly… flawed!

But sometimes life turns out for good, in ways we do not think!
When all, it seems, is dark and dense,
The light will brave a chink!
What once was crippling torment,
Is slowly turned to hope,
And what 'moved in' as crisis,
Now gives way to brighter scope!

BUT… now and then a wonderment, will break through all the black!
When all your world is crashing in,
God's hand will pull you back!
What once was just impossible,
Can all at once be true,
And what people say can't happen….
The Lord Himself will do!

OK! Fine! So maybe God exists…

PLEASE FOLLOW THE MIRACULOUS STORY OVER THE PAGE...

Funny how things turned out this time, THIS LIFE that looked so bleak...
(With talk or sure disaster...
And prospects, frail and weak)
Defied ALL given outcomes,
And LIVES to prove the fact,
That miracles do happen,
Even when the odds are stacked!

(Thank You Lord for Leo! – You healed him in the womb,
When man's determined prophecies,
Spoke only words of doom.
We dedicate him to You,
As his future now unfolds,
For Your grace is without limit...,
Like the destiny he holds!!

"A medical degree is something that I did not think I would need for my own journey through pregnancy and motherhood. But I had to learn a lot very quickly. Mostly though, I learnt FAITH…

… Leo was diagnosed in-vitro as having gastroschisis; when the bowel of the child is OUT of the body. According to every medical professional, this does not go back in after 13 weeks; hence I was categorically diagnosed at 13 weeks. The prognosis for this condition is not great—often with a fatal outcome.

… Along the pregnancy journey, I was then told that the diagnosis was now actually an omphalocele, which comes with chromosomal abnormalities—a worse and more worrying condition. After an amniocentesis, which was strongly requested in order to establish what chromosomal abnormalities there were, I was then later informed that the cultures had become infected, so that they were unable to give me the results of this vital diagnostic test. This is very rare! It was said to me at this time, that Leo may have club feet, heart defects or any one of many rare and often life-limiting chromosome defects. If indeed he survives.

"No" I thought. "Not this time, surely? This isn't meant to happen. This can't happen! My life will be undone and so will I if this happens", especially after losing the twins! So, after some strategizing over what to do, we started to pray.

We were the secret warrior trio. My Mum, Dr Anne (who was a retired obstetric surgeon) and me. We agreed and declared that this would not come to pass. We began to pray over Leo's life, but more importantly, we began to talk to Leo's spirit in the womb and started the process of instructing him and blessing him to partner with God and the Holy Spirit to receive His healing. It was a continual prayerful process to connect with Leo's spirit by speaking out loud to him through the walls of my tummy. Spirits have ears and are ageless, so we knew that the spirit given to Leo by God, was alive, mature and listening. We blessed and instructed. We declared and decreed. We exercised faith and spoke words of an alternative truth, even though that truth of healing was not yet visible in the physical realm. It was a difficult and stressful time, and holding the line of faith was not easy, especially because of our experience of the twins' shattering deaths. Yet, we kept on, in agreement and prayer. Every scan and assessment was attended by Dr Anne, who became the medical witness throughout my journey, and she was steadfast in that duty: diligent and watchful. As we journeyed, the in-vitro picture slowly started to change…..

OK! Fine! So maybe God exists…

After several weeks of unclear reports due to unhelpful foetal positioning, the medics finally saw something. They said that all that could be identified was a one cm defect at the navel. Gleeful at this, I turned to the sonographer and said "Well, that's good isn't it?". I waited for his response, sure in God that this was a good thing. He was non-committal and subdued and although all the measurements, metrics and various other assessments of growth and fluid etc. were all good, his expression was not in line with my upbeat question.

"We'll have to see what the senior paediatric surgeon says," he ventured "as medically, bowels do not go back in after 13 weeks".

"Well we have been praying," I said "...and I do believe in miracles. All other signs are positive aren't they? Nothing contra indicative?"

"No," he said, "All looks to be ok from the assessment, but as we know, bowels do not go back in after 13 weeks".

We waited for the top guy to come (sorry, Senior Paediatric Surgeon) and after some deliberation, he delivered his diagnosis and prognosis. It was the moment of ultimate challenge, faith versus professional pronouncement.

"Well, unfortunately," he said, "there is no medical precedent, ever, for a bowel going back in to the body, so the fact that there is only now a small defect at the navel, means that it is likely that the bowel has become detached from there—and probably disintegrated in the amniotic fluid, and therefore, it is probable that there is only half a bowel, and the bowel he has got, is ruptured".

As you can imagine a flurry of debate, opposition, questioning and clarification ensued, from which the outcome was that, although the 'top guy' insisted that he was right, ultimately, time would tell. It was there and then decided as a non-negotiable, that Leo's planned caesarean birth would not be allowed to take place without all relevant healthcare professionals present at the birth (about 8 different departments including surgeons, resuscitation team, neo natal, anaesthetists, midwives etc) and a reserved incubator in place ahead of the birth.

> We began to talk to Leo's spirit in the womb and started the process of instructing him and blessing him to partner with God and the Holy Spirit to receive his healing.

Other requests from myself to re-write the intended birth plan (which was currently imposed as removing the child from mother at birth for assessment), were to be taken up directly with the HEAD of Special Care at Sheffield Children's Hospital. This meant that I was going to have to fight in belief of my miracle, just a little bit more! I was both feet in for this one!

It turns out that the head honcho aforementioned was the same person who had been there and overseen the living and dying days of the twins and had been the person to keep bringing me the updates of the situation. He had brought the difficult life and death dilemmas to me and had brought Elliott to us in his dying hour, for us to say goodbye. Three times he brought him back, saying, " He isn't dead yet, he's not breathing, but his heart is still beating. He can still hear you as the hearing is the last sense to go, but we cannot take him to the mortuary until he is no longer alive". You get the picture. This guy had

been there at these dark moments, and for sure, he remembered me and he remembered the twins. I even think he remembered the pain and the agonising trauma…. he had been there and had shared in it.

So, I made an appointment to go and see him and began to seek God about my plan. Over a couple of days at home, I spent hours re-forming my birth plan based on positive expectation, and I exercised every inch and thread of my faith to believe that this was a plan that was going to be a reality, not a failed script for a play! It was a bit surreal, but clutching my bits of paper which represented the culmination of all the faith input from our secret warrior trio, I ventured to the meeting on the appointed day. Yes, he remembered me! Hallelujah for that!

> " I didn't feel afraid, I just had a deep sense of belief and faith that all would be well, and I reaffirmed my prayer that Leo would wee as soon as he was delivered.
> _____

After an emotional and candid meeting, in which I was thankfully made to feel cared for and important, it was agreed that my birth plan would be granted and

OK! Fine! So maybe God exists…

upheld as long as there was no contra-indication in respect of Leo's condition. Pivotally, if Leo were to come out and pass water or a stool, to prove that his bowel was joined up and nor ruptured, then this would make it easier for the professionals to follow my plan, without critical concern. That was good! Something to pray into.

During the final weeks of Leo's pregnancy, hope was strong and faith was hanging in alongside, so the day came and on 6/6/12 (which is in fact D –Day) Leo was coming into the world. In the hospital, the praying warrior team (Mum and Dr Anne) were on hand close by to the surgery table, and a large crowd of specialists waited no more than a few metres away, ready to pounce if needed. As delivery began by caesarean section, I felt a strong sense that everything was going to be ok. I didn't feel afraid, I just had a deep sense of belief and faith that all would be well, and I reaffirmed my prayer that Leo would wee as soon as he was delivered.

Yes, Hallelujah, as soon as Leo was pulled out, he passed urine straight away, and I knew this was a sign. Confused and certainly deciding not to mention the elephant in the room,

that all was in fact well (so far) the top guy decided to say to me, not "It's a miracle Mrs Doolan, your son is healed as you had suggested!" No! He said "Congratulations, your son was born at 12.12". I thought this very odd that he would say that. It had never been said to me before at any of my previous three birthing experiences. I said, "He's called Leo. His initials, each one remembering lost children"…. (Louis, Elliott & the Others—my four other miscarriages without names). He acknowledged this, but was distracted by the excitement of all that was going on, and by the obvious false alarm that was now hovering over the crowded delivery theatre. Yes, good word, this really was theatre! Theatre of God's making. Only later did I realise that the timing the Dr had mentioned rather unusually, was in fact, significant numerically and spiritually speaking— as Leo's birth date was 6/6/12 at 12.12. If he hadn't have said it, then I wouldn't have known. It was another unusual and significant detail of the miraculous tale.

….Anyway, back to the story….. They briefly whisked Leo away to make sure that he was breathing, and then, as per my birth plan detail, they brought him to me for bonding. Praise God! I had my Leo in my arms and he was ok.

No bowel defects, no tubes hanging out and no club feet. I checked his navel to make sure! I was shocked! I did a double take and looked confused at Dr Anne, who in her career as obstetric surgeon had delivered many babies into the world. She looked back at me equally shocked and looked baffled. At Leo's navel was a 2 cm bright yellow (and I mean like a marigold glove yellow) stump at the base of the umbilical cord. What on earth was that? Turns out, that was indeed the question! Perhaps not something from earth at all, but instead something heavenly. The surgeons had been so perplexed and thrown by this bright yellow 'thing' that they had all scratched their heads with no explanation at all between them. Not wanting to mess with something that could be bowel related, they cut the umbilical cord quite long so as not to take any chances or interfere with this phenomenon. So I asked Anne what it was, and she said that she didn't know, but that she was going to ask God about it. She did indeed ask God, although His reply came later when Anne was in her quiet time back at home. It was an answer that I'll never forget!!

He said to her " If I choose to put My Glory there, then what's that to you?" So, that made sense to me. God's miracle site, and He marked it with a bright yellow sign post! Of course! The yellow faded over the days and fell away with the rest of the umbilical cord, but this had cemented the idea of something special and significant in the minds of the medical team. Yet still, no-one mentioned the elephant in the room, that Leo was healthy and healed. They conducted all their tests over the following week—but despite all their medical notes, all their prognosis and every medical precedent…… they could not find anything wrong with Leo's bowel. They kept checking and kept head scratching, but could find no fault or flaw.

So, on the day of discharge from hospital, the Senior Registrar came and sat on my bed and brought my notes. He opened the flimsy backed report file, perusing it for a while, and clicked his pen a few times as he searched for what to say. "So," he said "How is Leo?" I waited before I responded. I paused and looked at him. He knew that I knew that this was a loaded question.

OK! Fine! So maybe God exists…

"I know that your notes may say differently," I said, "but he really is ok. Isn't he? And there is no other explanation for this than a miracle! He is a miracle!"
He looked at me and nodded, saying under his breath begrudgingly "I guess so."

I looked at him again with a kind of raised eyebrow expression, and ventured " I know you are reluctant to send me home because of what your notes say, but I have stayed in longer than needed, so that—as per my birth plan agreement—you could do all your tests….yet you have found nothing. He really is a miracle! You have to agree to send me home now and acknowledge this outcome".
So, he closed his book and with a defeated nod, he agreed to discharge me!!

And that was that! I guess my Top Guy, my Heavenly Father, really was a greater authority than their top guy! **He knew best and He answered our prayers! Amen!**

> **"**
> He really is a miracle! You have to agree to send me home now and acknowledge this outcome".
> So, he closed his book and with a defeated nod, he agreed to discharge me!!
> _____

The Wilderness

You're standing in the wilderness, its lonely and its cold,
No-one to bring you comfort, no-one for you to hold,
No real place of shelter, you're fragile and exposed,
It feels like you're forgotten and it seems like heaven's closed.
There's torment in the wandering; deception in the wait,
There's temptation from the enemy; no pathways that are straight.
There are whispers in your ear to wound and to confuse,
There are lies and then there's more lies to bewilder and bemuse.
You're holding tight to truth and faith, rehearsing words to say,
As darkness from the evil one encircles you as prey,
There's certain vulnerability on each and every side,
Nowhere to build a fortress, no place that You can hide.
No refuge and no sanctuary, just vast, foreboding land,
You don't know where to rest your head or even where to stand.
You're stumbling in self-pity, and fending-off despair,
You're hungry, weak and weary, and your hope is barely there.
Your mind is searching reason, and your soul is insecure,
Your body's screaming fear and your spirit's on the floor,
Your doubt is quickly rising and you really are not sure....
If you have a loving Saviour, *then what are you here for??*
You ask the Lord for answers; you beg Him to provide,
You cry out for a miracle, to strengthen you inside,
You search the sky for rescue and pray He'll pull you out,
But knelt in desperation, through tears, you finally shout....

"Lord, why's there no provision, and why unanswered prayer?
I need an explanation, for this seems so unfair!
Why have I lost Your favour? Why have You closed the door
To everything Your faithful child has simply asked You for?"

Then you remember Jesus, who was perfect in God's sight,
But he too walked the wilderness, forty days and forty nights.
Everything He there endured was hostile and unkind,
So what determined His response, what purpose did He find?

OK! Fine! So maybe God exists...

The Word of God prevailed, on His lips and in His heart,
A weapon forged divinely, from which truth cannot depart,
Though tempted there and tested, this weapon set Him free,
The spoken Truth so powerful, that the enemy let Him be.

So now I know my weapon was with me all along,
The Word of God my spear, and Praises for my tongue,
My Faith to be a shield and Truth to ward-off fear,
Despite my lack for everything, I know God's love is near.

I see this isn't punishment, it's just the Potter's hand,
He's shaping me for destiny, and all that He has planned,
He's more concerned with character, and if my heart is true,
He's watching my responses, not just my 'say and do'.

He's set a bridge for Kingdom's sake, to sift His remnant Bride,
And those with eyes on Him alone, will reach the other side.
Yes, Moses, John the Baptist and Jesus went before,
And came out with God's message, strong-rooted at their core.

I can survive this season, with all its fears and foes,
I can revive my reason.... and this is how it goes....
Though wilderness is harsh and tough, no choice but to contend,
My purpose from eternal scrolls awaits at season's end.

So here I am still standing, but my vision is now clear,
I see God's preparation and I know why I am here,
To wait for this new season as winter turns to spring....
Then take the World this message - of our soon returning King!

The Wilderness.   Howard Barnes

OK! Fine! So maybe God exists...

I literally feel like I lived in the wilderness of post trauma and 'destiny seeking' for years and years. Achingly long and frustrating, and desperately lonely at times. But God's timing is everything, although it is virtually impossible to see that from within the circumstance, I now see it more clearly. I appreciate how God moulds us in these dark places, and teaches us so much of what we need for our equipping and for the journey of faith. The wilderness is about learning to overcome and knowing the source of the overcoming.

The River

Come and be washed in the river, come and wade in as it flows,
There's healing released in the river, but you have to get in past your toes!

Come be refreshed in the river, don't just observe from the banks,
Your fuel gauge is running on empty, so come and replenish your tanks.

Come be submerged in the river, leave all inhibitions aside,
Come and receive peace abundant: let fear be released to the tide.

Come and jump in to the river, there's full restoration and rest,
There's no special costume or training… come as you are, fully dressed!

Come and just bathe in the river, there's love to uphold weary flesh,
Come be renewed and empowered – as the Spirit infills you afresh!

Come and submit to the river, for the Spirit is calling you in,
Receive of His gifts in their fullness… deposit all weakness and sin!

Come to the Spirit – the river! For He is the water that pours,
His mercy and healing are flowing, so do not be glued to the shores!

Wade in the Spirit's outpouring! Do not just watch from the edge,
His Spirit is coming in torrents, for this is His promise, His pledge!

Come be transformed in the river, The Spirit brings power divine,
It's source is the Lord, the Almighty, and this is a pivotal sign…

…The river will flow from The Temple, The Church, His Apostles, His Own!
So do not miss out on The Glory, for its coming from God's Holy Throne.

Come and have life in the river; be healed, be strengthened, be free!!
It's a flow that will carry you always… **and will lead to the Heavenly Sea!**

OK! Fine! So maybe God exists…

 I have had to spend quite a bit of time in the River—or for those that don't know—in the presence of God where the anointing of the Holy Spirit is flowing and ministering. It's soaking yourself in His glory, His love, His grace, His blessing and His healing and its being willing to swim in these waters for a while.

The River is free and it never runs dry, but like wild swimming or cold sea swimming, you have to just get in, even if it's a bit uncomfortable at first, for you to feel the myriad of benefits to body, soul and spirit.

END TIME DAYS ARE HERE...

Well here we are in 'end times'! Is this how it's meant to feel?
I guess I thought this season would be slightly more surreal!
I expected something freaky, like a movie or a show…...
But we're here at such a juncture, and the World still doesn't know!

I've often truly thought of it, how would this time play out?
Romanticed an epic cast, with my role not in doubt.
A little bit of witnessing, and a miracle or two…...
I've seen it in my thought life: hoped I'd know just what to do!

Yet here we are in prophesy with the earth a total mess!
The powers are grabbing ever more, and our freedom's ever less!
The written things from Scripture are happening in our face….
But we're mostly just still trudging on, this hoodwinked human race!

It's not like I imagined, where somehow evil's guise,
Would be seen by 'all and sundry' and they'd call-out all its lies,
But things could not be further from these musings of my mind,
We're largely in 'cloud cuckoo land', with people's eyes still blind.

But this is what God talked of, with many men deceived,
Despite his flagrant warnings, He has not been believed!
The job done on humanity by leaders and elite,
Is a long-play brainwash strategy and it's nearly now complete.

We're born to some society where we're made to think we're free,
We're fed a bunch of half-baked truths which we take on willingly.
We don't know any better as a false construct is sold,
But our God giv'n rights and divine insights have been locked up in their 'hold'.

OK! Fine! So maybe God exists...

But the keys have now been shaken and the 'hold' has lost its jaws,
The fake and flawed society is a surely fading cause,
The sham of rotten science and a world that pushed out Christ,
Can no longer mask its evil and not all are so enticed!

For those that know this portent, God's prophecy and plans,
This end time game is futile, for God's hand outplays all man's!
It's not a global reset at the hands of evil men,
No, it's God's great Kingdom reset, where He'll come to earth again!

There's much the World will witness in the crossfire of this war,
When evil has a given stretch to implement its law,
But Christ will thwart that kingdom as His sovereign rule awaits,
And He'll enter to Jerusalem by the City's Golden Gates.

But can you dare believe it, we're here at those end times?
The anti-Christ will hasten and the tribulation chimes!
A marriage feast will happen in the air for those that wait,
And a judgment seat is coming where the world will meet its fate.

It's all laid out quite clearly in the book we people read,
The Bible tells of all of this, though many do not heed.
Do not be caught-out sleeping in the lies that man has made,
'Cos end time days are here, and it's time you sought and prayed.

Yes, end time days are here and it isn't like I thought.
There isn't a big drum roll and a villain that gets caught.
No this is pure deception, but it's real and in The Book….
If you're in doubt, then take time out, and go and have a look….. !!!

... Remember, I am with you always to the end of the ages ...

OK! Fine! So maybe God exists...

I have known and seen where this world is headed for most of my life. I'm not psychic and its not some secret I've been privy to….. no, it's because its all in the bible! I've been telling people for years, BUT now we are actually here. If you are, what is termed as 'asleep'- in other words, not aware of any of this because you live your life without seeing the bigger picture or challenging media fodder— then this poem may be one of two things. Either a head spinning eye-opener, OR a meaningless word jumble that has left you perplexed. Its time folks! Please look, see and prepare….

I'M PRAYING FOR AN UPGRADE

I'm praying for an upgrade, dear Lord that I may be,
Entwined with heaven's mandate and joined up with destiny.
I'm praying for an upgrade Lord, so I can now fulfil,
My purpose and commission and Your long established Will.
What do I need to qualify for end time servanthood?
Do I need certain qualities that You would see as good?
Would I meet Your criteria for taking on this role?
I feel that I could do it Lord……. live out what's on my scroll!

I'm praying for an upgrade Lord, to be a 'Dunamite',
A wielder of Your power and an agent of Your Might!
I'm praying for an upgrade Lord, to draw the Spirit's flame,
Where deaf will hear, where blind will see and out will walk the lame!
I know Your strength and power Lord, I know You hold all keys,
I know Your breath or shadow, can bring men to their knees.
I want to be a vessel Lord, from which Your deeds can flow,
I want to pray and move Your hand, that all may see and know.

I'm praying for an upgrade Lord to effect a gathering in,
A harvest time of lost and found all washed clean from their sin,
I'm praying for an upgrade Lord, so I can be Your voice,
To boldly preach salvation, and see hundreds make that choice.
I'd love the opportunity, the boldness and the chance,
To sing Your praise to thousands and see kingdom souls advance,
I long for more appointments and for doors to open wide,
Where I could tell my story Lord…. show how I'm justified.

I'm praying for an upgrade Lord, to make all demons fear,
To speak with Your authority, and they will disappear.
I'm praying for an upgrade Lord, so satan has no play,
I'll speak Your name, to stop his game and he will cower away!
I want to stop tormentors, to roar and they will go!
I want to scare the enemy, so people here will know,
That You alone are sovereign and Your Kingship is supreme,
Let all oppressed be loosened and Your cleansing power redeem.

OK! Fine! So maybe God exists...

I'm praying for an upgrade Lord, that I may raise the dead,
And that's not wishful thinking, for that's something You have said!
I'm praying for an upgrade Lord, that I could just be more.......
To heal the sick, and free the bound and satisfy the poor.
So I'm praying for an upgrade Lord, to come before too long!
I want the World to know You through my testament and song,
I'm praying for an upgrade so the gifts You've placed in me,
Can do the heavenly business and can change eternity.

I know I might sound greedy Lord, by wanting all these things,
But I'm longing for Your Kingdom come and all this season brings.
I long to see the "who I am" be purposed in this time,
And my spirit longs to prosper and be living in its prime.
But Lord if all that's coming is an upgrade in Your sight,
Then Father I'll be satisfied to be a brighter light,
And I would change my wishlist to be far more circumspect,
And I'd like to add these upgrades to be overseen and checked.....

I'd like a bit more wisdom and some clarity and peace.
I'd like to be in total strength with body pain released.
I'd like some more humility and more anointing too,
Discernment, faith and vision with a clear prophetic view.
I'd like more understanding, more resilience and more grace.
More love to give out freely and more time to seek Your face,
A little more forgiveness and more purity of heart....
A know I still need more dear Lord, but this is just a start!

So I'm praying for an upgrade Lord, whatever that may be,
To stand up and be counted and to give the best of me,
To get to know You better and to trust You come what may,
For the upgrade that's eternal, will be coming ...... any day!!

These are my means of that upgrade

OK! Fine! So maybe God exists...

Am I the finished article? No definitely not! There are big things coming down the line for which God has given us the script in the bible. Well, I don't know about you, but if I know there's something coming, I want to be prepared. God's showdown is in the next chapter of time, and I am firmly in the winning camp—so here's where I want my life to count for something that will be recorded in the annals of eternity, "The Lamb's Book of Life! (Rev. 13:8)

Chapter 6

God wants to speak...

I AM THE GREAT I AM

My dearest, warrior remnant, My fragrant, holy bride,
I'm looking to upgrade you, come up! Be set aside!
But I am needing greater, deeper trust in who I Am,
For surely, I'm omniscient! The Lion and the Lamb!

I am Jehovah Rapha, your Healer and your King.
I am Jehovah Jireh, your provider in all things.
I am , most surely Adonai; My rule all powers transcend!
I'm Alpha and Omega - Beginning and the End.

I am refreshing rainfall, I come in heavenly showers.
I am a holy presence, with awesome, fearsome powers.
I am a burning fire, with heat and force I fall,
I am a rushing, surging wind, on which you'll hear My call.

I am the gentle Ruach, the breath of God complete.
I am your Great Deliverer, who does not know defeat.
I am the Key of Promise, My Word is pure and true,
I am the Lord of Heavenly Hosts, to whom all praise is due.

I am the lifter of your head, when you are battle weak.
I am your strength and utterance who gives you words to speak
I am your shield, protector - whose Name makes demons flee.
I am the Lover of Your Soul, through all eternity.

I am the Good Samaritan who tends your every need.
I am Divine Creator, who planned and made your seed.
I am a peace so precious; the World can't understand,
I am a loving Father, and I hold you in My hand.

OK! Fine! So maybe God exists...

I am your light in darkness, when you have lost your way.
I am your strength and purpose, when all your clouds seem grey.
I'm loving arms around you, when pain is in your heart,
And I mend the broken-hearted: repairing every part.

I am the Mighty Prophet; all knowledge mine to share.
I am all truth and wisdom; too perfect to compare.
I am divine anointing that ordains the gifts you hold,
I'm giver of all authority, to fulfill what's on your scroll.

I am much more than Great I Am; I'm Yahweh Elohim!
What needs can I not satisy? From Me all mercies stream!
I'm Grace and Mercy endless and a covenant at your side,
I'm always ever with you - let all these truths reside!

As battle rages stronger, and darkness presses in,
You have to know "THE GREAT I AM", for only then, you'll win.
Come up to deeper trusting, to living out My Word,
Rise up to faith unwaver'ing; don't feint or be deterred.

Its time for higher purpose, its time to rise above.
Its time to cast out fear and doubt; be anchored in My Love.
Its time to let your spirits be positioned at the fore,
Aligned to Kingdom living, and drawn-out more and more.

These whispers are not secrets, but many will not hear,
So I'm sharing My heart with you, and making My words clear,
"Rise up" in truth of all I Am, "rise up" to Kingdom's ways!
For your trials are preparations, for the coming Glory Days!

OK! Fine! So maybe God exists...

Well. Although I wrote these words, as a scribe writes on behalf of someone else, so these words are not mine. God often imparts to and through me, words He wants to say. It's an awesome responsibility to communicate and present God's words, but He has entrusted me with this gift. Its only because I have 'borne the very depths of grief a human heart can bear and yet remained true to Him', that He gave and entrusted this unique gift.

It comes to me in thoughts, words, rhythm and tone... much of it already formed. The gift expresses it all in metre and rhyme and chooses vocabulary, but essentially, it comes from the spirit to the pen.

Please read these divine words and know they are not from my own imagination, but from the heart of God.

If Only You Knew...

If only you knew how My heart breaks, when man blames Me for his mistakes …
As fists are waved for floods and quakes… he doesn't see the path he takes…
Let Me confide how My soul aches………………

I, the God that made your frame
And know each one by deed and name,
Have not with spite and random aim,
Unleashed a bitter, judgement game.
The darkness you invited in,
Has made a way for reckless sin,
And torment with its knowing grin
Has waged a war, intent to win.
So do not label Me "unfair",
I have not planned the earth's despair,
I love you all and deeply care,
That's why your rage is hard to bear.

IF ONLY YOU KNEW this Father's pain, why am I held in such disdain? ….
By those for whom My Son was slain… I would He had not died in vain…
But please allow Me to explain…………………..

Why is it you've rejected Me?
I gave My Son so willingly,
To suffer death at Calvary,
And gain your lost eternity.
I paid the highest price for you,
My heart ripped out and rent in two.
What more is it you'd have Me do,
To prove this Father's love is true?
Rejection's sting has dealt its blow,
More harshly than you'll ever know,
And as I sit in pain and woe,
It's still My grace and love that flow.

OK! Fine! So maybe God exists...

If only you knew the depth of grief, to which your praise brings blessed relief…
It pools its tears a way beneath… to mourn My Israel's unbelief…
But hear your God, in plain, in brief…………….........

My Israel through these ages past,
You've always been, My first, My last,
My love's so rich, so deep, so vast,
Complete and total, unsurpassed.
Yet history's shown this love is spurned:
Unrequited, unreturned:
But a Father's love is free, not earned,
It has never wavered, never turned.
So, every time you're torn apart,
As wolves have struck with deadly art,
I've cried your pain inside My heart,
With endless tears that sear and smart.
If only you knew the tears I've shed, over unmarked graves with thousands dead…
As half the world is underfed… and I watch as man with man is wed…
Just let Me share what's yet unsaid………………

Sometimes I dare not turn My face,
Toward My kin, the human race,
Affliction mocks in ev'ry place
And waywardness touts hell's disgrace.
Your suffering has plagued My door,
The lost, the sick, the sad, the poor,
And whilst My hurt is fresh and raw,
You trounce My ways and wound Me more.
I weep for those that live in fear,
Just hoping you may let Me near,
But things grow darker year on year,
As I wait for you… My World…. I'm here!

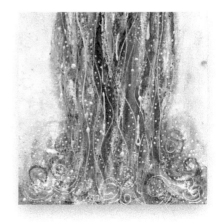

I long that all may be restored,
Your destiny, once more assured,
My Church, My Bride in one accord,
And I, again, your King and Lord.
Unprotected, broken, scared:
My Israel, hope has yet been spared,
For that which evil's hand has dared,
Cannot confound what I've prepared.
A coming home, a wedding feast,
Where you the greatest; you the least,
From north and south and west and east,
Will reign with Me: enriched, increased!

If only you knew how sorrow's hand, has tainted many blessings planned…
I share your pain, each vein, each strand…
I bring this so you'll understand…

IF ONLY YOU KNEW…
IF ONLY YOU KNEW…
MAYBE ONE DAY YOU'LL KNOW…

God's heart is broken! Doubt it not! The fall and
subversion of the human race away from HIS design
and the utter rejection (for the most part) of the
sacrifice of His Son, have left God in anguish. But God
is no fool—His plan to restore all of creation will and
cannot be stopped. It is coming soon as the decline
of humanity reaches its ultimate fall….

OK! Fine! So maybe God exists…

Tears in heaven ...

GOD OF THE BREAKTHROUGH

I know that your hearts here are heavy,
I know that you're troubled in mind,
I know there's more questions than answers,
And I know that these days are unkind.

I know you have lost those you cherish,
I know that you're hurt and confused,
I know that your prayers grow impatient,
And I know that your faith has been bruised.

I know that you're tired of your worries,
I know that you're desperate for peace,
I know that your bodies are weary,
And I know that your battles increase.

I know that your families are shaken,
I know that your strength has been sapped,
I know that you see much to fear,
And I know that so many feel trapped.

BUT, I am the Lord God of Israel,
Your Mighty, Victorious King,
And I will not ever desert you,
For I cradle you under My wing.

I know life has treated you cruelly,
I know that the season is black,
I know people feel frustrated,
For it seems there is nothing but lack.

BUT, I am your Father in Heaven,
And all that you see I have made,
I know the end and beginning,
So 'My Own', you should not be afraid.

OK! Fine! So maybe God exists...

I call you to hold your faith tightly,
I call you to lay its roots deep,
Just cling to the rock that is Jesus,
And look to My face as you weep.

I weep with you also, for Israel,
Their plight has provoked Me to act,
So your time and their time have junctured,
And tell all your leaders this fact!

Yes, all around you may crumble,
The earth may be rocked to its core,
The world may collapse under crisis,
And nations speak murder and war.

BUT, do not give up 'midst disaster,
Be not despondent and weak,
Lay down confusion and trembling,
Surrender your doubt as I speak!

I am the God of the Breakthrough,
I have My all-conquering plan,
I'm depending on you to out-play it,
And that's why this test is on man.

God is a personal God. He
knows and cares about our
circumstances. He also knows
about the frustration and
angst of those that know the
light and feel they are battling
against the dark. God here
offers reassurances about both
His love and concern, and His
plan to break through all the
World's shambolic evil mess.

Stand on My Word and keep righteous,
Be most alert in this hour,
This time of great trial and struggle,
Has shown Me My army of power.

I am the Omega and Alpha,
So hear this as strength to your soul,
I will make a way in the darkness,
I Am still the God in control!

NEVER BEYOND REACH

You might think your sinfulness is way beyond My care,
You might believe your errant life is too far past repair,
You might engage with age-old lies that say you have no worth,
BUT I have watched and beckoned since you first took form on earth.

You might believe your darkened thoughts have pushed you wide and far,
You might have ditched your innocence that once framed who you are,
You might believe your failures-all have meant you're lost to Me....
BUT you are never out of reach; I look, I know, I see!

You may regret your secret things and ways you have behaved,
You might believe these acts and deeds mean you cannot be saved,
You might assume there's no return from shame and guilt and crime,
BUT I the God that made you, have loved you for all time.

You might rehearse mistaken thoughts that drown out truth you've known,
You may now say your human form is all you have and own,
You might, now think your flesh and bone will take you through the veil...
BUT your spirit is eternal and your human flesh will fail.

You may excuse and justify the path that you have trod,
You try hard to convince yourself that you are your own 'god',
You may cling-fast to false beliefs that say I am not real...
BUT I Am sole Creator and your breath is still My seal.

I see your disappointment, your sadness and your grief,
It's quashed the faith that lived in you and crushed all your belief.
I see your pitted journey and the dark that's filled your soul...
BUT I am still here loving you with plans to make you whole.

Whilever there is life in you, before all judgement lands,
There's nothing that can put you out beyond My loving hands,
There's nothing that can set you back beyond My reaching gaze,
There's not one soul beyond all grace in earth's remaining days.

OK! Fine! So maybe God exists...

This was written with a few people in mind; people I hold close to my heart and always in my consciousness. As I was mulling over the variety of circumstances from which God can draw people back to Him and how He can rescue flailing lives from the brink of negative spiral.…. God gave me this. Written quite unexpectedly and in a very short time, this was the key assurance that I know He wanted people to hear. There is ALWAYS a way back to God and to salvation.

There is no separation that can over-reach My love,
There is no place of hiding that escapes My throne above,
There is no layered blackness from which you cannot be free,
For Jesus died to save you and repentance is the key.

My plan is for redemption, for freedom and for gain,
The sacrifice was Christ My Son, as He was charged and slain,
But as He rose in victory, your sin was fully paid…
You only need accept this, and the ruling lies will fade.

You're not beyond forgiveness, you're not beyond My light!
But always life is tricky: it's a journey and a fight!
So I am ever longing to restore, redeem and teach….
My love and grace await you; I am never beyond reach!

The Door to Life

A door is mapped out for the seeker,
A passage to life for each soul,
Our time on this earth is to find it,
Less sin and self-love take their toll.
We have to be sure of our purpose,
To not just discover the door,
But to earnestly knock and go through it,
To establish what this life is for!
Inaction will not move you forward,
The need to 'step out' is on you,
So knock on the door and be mindful,
Don't put-off your chance to go through!

Do not miss your chance to go through the door of salvation. Do not miss your chance to find your heavenly eternity. Do not miss your chance to secure the future and safety of your soul.......

"Knock and the door will be opened to you"

THE END

OK! Fine! So maybe God exists...

Acknowledgements

COPYRIGHT	©2023 Dovetail Music	**FRONT COVER**	Howard Barnes
ISBN	978-1-910848-55-5 All rights reserved.	**BACK COVER PHOTO**	Lucy Jones Photography
POETRY	Juliet Dawn	**DESIGN**	rocketpixels.co.uk
ARTWORK	Howard Barnes, Lizzie Westhead and Barbie Hunt		

Resources

Dovetail Shalom have a large catalogue of resources to bless and encourage people on their life journey. These include:

- Studio worship albums (various CDs)
- Selection of poetry books
- Numerous teaching CDs
- Film DVD of Pilgrims Progress and it's associated music CD and study book

 www.dovetailshalom.co.uk to view and order

 dovetailshalom@gmail.com for further assistance with enquiries.

 Dovetail Shalom to connect with video content and online events.

Dovetail Shalom host a **weekly zoom** meeting on Fridays with guest speakers, prayer, worship and topical conversation.

Please contact Brenda Taylor **via email for ID and password.**

The Prayer of Salvation

This is possibly the most important page in the book.... not one to skip past if you care about your eternal future and destiny.

Here is a prayer you can say to accept Jesus as your Saviour, and start a wonderful eternal destiny.

Dear Heavenly Father
I truly want to belong to You, and realise I am a sinner and need your forgiveness.
I believe that Jesus died for me, taking on Himself the punishment I deserve.
Please cleanse my heart and come and live in me, so I can walk and talk with You in a love relationship.
Thank you that this is what I was created for and now I have eternal life, through Christ Jesus, my Saviour and Lord.
Amen

For God so loved the one world that He gave His only-begotten Son, that all who believe in Him should not perish, but have eternal life.

JOHN 3:16

OK! Fine! So maybe God exists...

BV - #0087 - 110923 - C132 - 210/148/9 - PB - 9781910848555 - Gloss Lamination